AF249398

LIFE Magic MASTERY for Moms

K P WEAVER

Copyright © K P Weaver

First published in Australia in 2022
by MMH Presss
Waikiki, WA 6169

All rights reserved. No part of this book may be used or reproduced by any means, graphic, electronic, or mechanical, including photocopying, recording, taping or by any information storage retrieval system without the written permission of the copyright owner except in the case of brief quotations embodied in critical articles and reviews.

Because of the dynamic nature of the Internet, any web addresses or links contained in this book may have changed since publication and may no longer be vaild. The views expressed in this work are solely those of the author and do not necessarily reflect the views of the publisher and the publisher hereby disclaims any responsibility for them.

Cover design by Ida Jensson

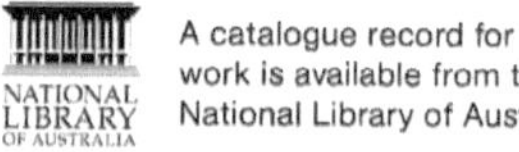

A catalogue record for this work is available from the National Library of Australia

National Library of Australia Catalogue-in-Publication data:

Life Magic Mastery for Moms/K P Weaver

ISBN:

(Paperback)

ISBN:

(Ebook)

CONTENTS

INTRODUCTION

Motherhood is a gift for us all to embrace not control

Motherhood is a journey like no other, a path filled with boundless love, immeasurable joy and transformative growth. It is a sacred role that carries with it the power to shape lives, nurture souls and create a lasting legacy. Yet, amidst the beauty and wonder of motherhood, there are also challenges, doubts and moments of uncertainty. In this extraordinary journey, we seek to uncover the hidden magic that lies within each mother, waiting to be awakened and embraced.

In this compilation of chapters, we delve into the depths of motherhood, exploring its many facets, complexities and profound moments of connection. From the universal laws that guide mothers with unwavering dedication to the practical tools and practices that enable them to embrace their role with grace, each chapter invites you on a transformative exploration of the magic that resides within motherhood.

Within these pages, you will embark on a journey of self-discovery and empowerment, as we unravel the threads of life magic that weave through the intricate tapestry of motherhood. We will explore the fundamental principles that govern the universe of motherhood, from the unyielding force of unconditional love to the power of forgiveness, gratitude and mindful presence. These universal laws serve as a compass, guiding mothers towards a more fulfilling, purpose-driven and heart-centred approach to their role.

As we venture deeper into this exploration, we will uncover the seven master gifts that lie within every mother waiting to be harnessed and expressed. These gifts encompass the essence of life magic: love, intuition, gratitude, forgiveness, self-belief, mindfulness and the power of intention. Through understanding and cultivating these gifts, mothers can tap into their innate potential and create transformative experiences for themselves and their children.

Moreover, we will witness the extraordinary capacity of mothers to serve as guardians of love, nurturing an environment of growth, resilience and self-discovery. By embracing their role as leaders, mentors and nurturers, mothers can cultivate deep connections, instil positive values and guide their children towards a future of limitless possibilities.

Throughout these chapters, we will celebrate the diversity of motherhood, exploring different cultural perspectives, expectations and practices. From African communal nurturing to Eastern principles of balance, from Indian devotion to indigenous wisdom, we will witness the enchanting tapestry of motherhood across the globe. Each culture brings forth its own unique rituals, beliefs and traditions, revealing the profound influence of heritage and the universal threads that connect all mothers.

In this quest for life magic mastery, we also acknowledge the significance of self-care and self-nurturing for mothers. By tending to their own wellbeing, mothers can replenish their spirits, cultivate resilience and find balance amidst the demands of their role. We will delve into the practices of mindful self-care, embracing the power of presence and nurturing their own dreams and aspirations.

So, whether you are a mother embarking on this magical journey, an expectant mother preparing for the arrival of a precious soul or someone who wishes to honour and appreciate the mothers in your life, this compilation of chapters holds something special for you. It is an invitation to awaken the magic within motherhood, to embrace the limitless possibilities that lie within and to celebrate the profound impact of mothers on the world.

As we embark on this transformative exploration together, may you find inspiration, guidance and empowerment within these pages. May you discover the boundless love, strength and wisdom that reside within you, waiting to be embraced and shared with the world. And may you come to realise that the magic of motherhood is not only a gift bestowed upon you but a force that emanates from deep within your heart.

Awakening

Awakening the magic within motherhood begins with the understanding and application of the universal laws.

AWAKENING THE MAGIC WITHIN MOTHERHOOD

Motherhood, with its many joys and challenges, is a transformative journey that holds within it the power to awaken the magic within us. It is a sacred path that beckons us to step into our fullest potential, embracing the profound role of nurturing, guiding and shaping the lives of our children. Yet, amidst the daily demands and responsibilities, it is easy to lose sight of the enchantment that exists within motherhood.

This book, *Life Magic Mastery for Moms,* is an invitation to embark on a journey of rediscovery and empowerment. It is a guide that seeks to unlock the hidden treasures and infinite possibilities that lie within the realm of motherhood. Within these pages, we will explore the profound influence of the universal laws and the seven life principles of mindfulness, knowing, intention, love, gratitude, forgiveness and belief.

Awakening the magic within motherhood begins with the understanding and application of the universal laws. These laws, such as the law of attraction, the law of cause and effect and the law of abundance, govern the fabric of our existence. By aligning ourselves with these laws, we tap into a wellspring of infinite potential, manifesting joy, abundance and fulfilment in our lives and the lives of our children.

Central to this journey is the cultivation of mindfulness. In the midst of the chaotic and fast-paced nature of motherhood, mindfulness allows us to be fully present, embracing each moment with grace and intention. Through mindfulness, we create a deep connection with ourselves, our children and the world around us. It becomes the foundation upon which we build our magical experiences as mothers.

Knowing, our inner wisdom and intuition, becomes our guiding compass. As mothers, we possess an innate knowing that transcends logic and reasoning. It is a profound wisdom that allows us to navigate the complexities of motherhood with grace and authenticity. By embracing and trusting our inner knowing, we make choices that align with our deepest truths and create a harmonious and fulfilling motherhood experience.

Intention becomes the fuel that ignites our desires and aspirations. By setting powerful intentions, we become conscious creators of our reality. With clarity and focus, we shape our motherhood journey, manifesting the experiences, connections and growth that aligns with our heart's deepest desires.

Love, the most powerful force in the universe, infuses every aspect of motherhood. It is through love that we connect, nurture and guide our children. Love becomes the cornerstone upon which we build strong foundations of trust, support and compassion. It is a super fuel that propels us to go beyond our limitations, fostering an environment of growth and authenticity.

Gratitude becomes a life hack, a key that unlocks the flow of abundance and joy. By cultivating gratitude, we shift our focus to the blessings and miracles that abound in our lives. Gratitude opens our hearts to the beauty and magic of each moment, enabling us to find contentment and fulfilment amidst the challenges and responsibilities of motherhood.

Forgiveness, both for ourselves and others, becomes a transformative tool. As mothers, we may encounter moments of frustration, guilt and resentment. Through forgiveness, we release these burdens, freeing ourselves and our children from the weight of past mistakes and grievances. Forgiveness becomes an act of liberation, creating space for healing, growth and deeper connections.

Belief becomes the foundation upon which we build our motherhood journey. By embracing empowering beliefs, we shatter limiting beliefs and embrace the infinite possibilities that exist within ourselves and our children. Belief becomes the catalyst for transformation, inspiring us to rise above challenges, embrace our strengths and nurture the potential that resides within us.

As you embark on this journey of life magic mastery, remember that motherhood is not merely a role we fulfil, but a sacred calling that invites us to harness our inner magic and create a world of love, joy and possibility for ourselves and our children.

AWAKENING THE MAGIC WITHIN: ENCOURAGING YOUR CHILDREN TO EMBRACE LIFE'S WONDERS

As mothers, we have the incredible opportunity to inspire and guide our children in discovering the magic of life. Encouraging them to embrace the wonders that surround them can cultivate a sense of awe, curiosity and appreciation for the world they inhabit. In this chapter, we explore how we can foster a mindset of magic and wonder in our children's lives.

AWAKENING THE SENSES

The magic of life is often experienced through our senses. Encourage your children to engage their senses fully, to notice the beauty of colours, the sounds of nature, the textures of objects and the tastes of different foods. Take them on sensory adventures, whether it's stargazing on a clear night, feeling the grass beneath their bare feet or listening to the symphony of birdsong in the early morning. By awakening their senses, we open their eyes to the enchantment that exists in everyday moments.

CULTIVATING WONDER AND CURIOSITY

Children are naturally curious beings, eager to explore and discover. Nurture their innate sense of wonder by encouraging questions, fostering a spirit of curiosity and providing opportunities for exploration. Create a sense of adventure by going on nature walks, visiting museums or engaging in imaginative play. Encourage them to ask questions, seek answers and embrace the joy of discovery. By cultivating wonder and curiosity, we nurture a lifelong love for learning and a deep appreciation for the mysteries of life.

EMBRACING THE POWER OF IMAGINATION

Imagination is a gateway to the magical realms of possibility. Encourage your children to unleash their imagination through storytelling, pretend play and creative endeavours. Provide them with the tools and resources to express their inner worlds, whether it's through drawing, writing or building. Support their imaginative play and join them in their magical adventures. By embracing the power of imagination, we open up endless possibilities and ignite their creative spark.

CONNECTING WITH NATURE'S MAGIC

Nature is a wellspring of magic and wonder. Encourage your children to develop a deep connection with the natural world. Take them on nature hikes, teach them about the life cycles of plants and animals and instil in them a sense of environmental stewardship. Show them the awe-inspiring beauty of sunsets, the intricate patterns of leaves and the delicate dance of butterflies. By connecting with nature's magic, we teach our children to appreciate the interconnectedness of all living things and the importance of nurturing our planet.

DISCOVERING EVERYDAY MIRACLES

Magic exists not only in extraordinary moments but also in the everyday miracles that surround us. Help your children develop a keen eye for spotting these small wonders. Encourage them to find joy in a blooming flower, a kind gesture from a stranger or a beautiful sunset. Teach them to appreciate the moments of serendipity, synchronicity and unexpected surprises that make life truly magical. By discovering everyday miracles, we cultivate a sense of gratitude and a deeper appreciation for the simple joys in life.

INSTILLING A BELIEF IN POSSIBILITY

Belief is the fuel that powers the magic of life. Nurture your children's belief in themselves and their dreams. Encourage them to pursue their passions, set goals and persevere in the face of challenges. Teach them that they have the power to create their own magic through determination, hard work and a positive mindset. By instilling a belief in possibility, we empower our children to embrace their unique potential and make their dreams a reality.

In conclusion, by encouraging our children to embrace the magic of life, we awaken their senses, cultivate wonder and curiosity, embrace the power of imagination, connect with nature's magic, discover everyday miracles and instil a belief in possibility. As mothers, we have the privilege to guide them on a journey of enchantment and help them see the extraordinary in the ordinary. Let us inspire them to live with wide-eyed wonder, knowing that life's magic is always within their reach.

Universal Thinking

Our actions, thoughts and emotions have a ripple effect that extends far beyond ourselves and our children.

UNDERSTANDING THE UNIVERSAL LAWS

A foundation for life mastery

In the vast tapestry of existence, there are certain laws that govern the workings of the universe. These laws, often referred to as the universal laws, are the underlying principles that shape our reality and influence every aspect of our lives. By understanding and aligning ourselves with these laws, we unlock the keys to life mastery and unlock the full potential that lies within us. In this chapter, we will delve into the fundamental universal laws and explore their profound implications for our journey as mothers.

THE LAW OF ATTRACTION: LIKE ATTRACTS LIKE

The law of attraction states that like attracts like. Simply put, the energy we put out into the world through our thoughts, emotions and actions attracts corresponding experiences and circumstances into our lives. As mothers, we have the power to shape our reality by consciously directing our thoughts and emotions. By cultivating positive and empowering thoughts, we invite abundance, joy and fulfilment into our motherhood journey.

THE LAW OF CAUSE AND EFFECT: ACTIONS AND CONSEQUENCES

The law of cause and effect, also known as the law of karma, states that every action has a corresponding consequence. Our thoughts, words and deeds create energetic ripples that reverberate throughout the universe. As mothers, our choices and actions not only impact our own lives but also leave an indelible imprint on the lives of our children. By understanding this law, we become conscious creators, mindful of the consequences of our choices and the example we set for our children.

THE LAW OF DIVINE ONENESS: INTERCONNECTEDNESS OF ALL

The law of divine oneness affirms that everything in the universe is interconnected and part of a unified whole. As mothers, we recognise that we are not separate entities, but rather integral parts of a greater web of life. Our actions, thoughts and emotions have a ripple effect that extends far beyond ourselves and our children. By embracing this law, we cultivate compassion, empathy and a sense of responsibility for the wellbeing of all beings.

THE LAW OF ABUNDANCE: EMBRACING A MINDSET OF PLENTY

The law of abundance teaches us that the universe is infinitely abundant, and there is more than enough for everyone. As mothers, we sometimes fall into the trap of scarcity thinking, believing that there is a limited supply of love, resources or opportunities. However, by aligning ourselves with the law of abundance, we shift our mindset to one of gratitude and trust in the abundant flow of life. We recognise that there is an abundance of love, support and opportunities available to us and our children.

THE LAW OF VIBRATION: EVERYTHING IS ENERGY

The law of vibration asserts that everything in the universe, including our thoughts and emotions, vibrates at a specific frequency. This vibrational energy attracts similar frequencies into our lives. As mothers, we can raise our energetic vibration by cultivating positive emotions such as love, joy and gratitude. By aligning our vibrations with our desires, we become magnetic to the experiences and opportunities that resonate with our highest good.

THE LAW OF CORRESPONDENCE: INNER AND OUTER WORLDS

The law of correspondence states that there is a correspondence between our inner world of thoughts, beliefs and emotions, and our outer world of experiences. As mothers, we understand that our thoughts and beliefs shape our perception of reality, influencing our interactions with our children and the world around us. By cultivating self-awareness and consciously choosing empowering thoughts and beliefs, we transform our inner world, which, in turn, reflects in our outer experiences.

THE LAW OF DIVINE TIMING: TRUSTING THE UNIVERSE'S PLAN

The law of divine timing reminds us that everything happens in perfect timing and order. As mothers, we may sometimes feel impatient or overwhelmed, longing for certain outcomes or milestones. However, by aligning ourselves with this law, we surrender to the flow of life and trust that everything unfolds at the right time. We let go of control and embrace the present moment, knowing that each stage of motherhood holds its own beauty and lessons.

Understanding and integrating these universal laws into our lives as mothers provides a powerful foundation for life mastery. By aligning ourselves with these principles, we become conscious creators of our reality, shaping our experiences and nurturing a harmonious and abundant motherhood journey.

In the following chapters, we will explore how these universal laws intersect with the seven life principles of mindfulness, knowing, intention, love, gratitude, forgiveness and belief. Through practical exercises, insights and real-life examples, we will delve deeper into each of these principles, uncovering their transformative potential in the context of motherhood.

I am a great believer that knowledge is key to success and taking time to understand and embrace the universal laws means that we can open our minds in faith and possibility.

Why not choose to step into our power as conscious creators, weaving the threads of magic, love and abundance into the tapestry of our lives and the lives of our children. Together, we will unlock the extraordinary potential that lies within motherhood and create a life filled with joy, purpose and fulfilment.

At the very core of a mother's being lies an unyielding wellspring of unconditional love.

THE UNIVERSAL LAWS
OF MOMS

Fuelled by a mission to serve

In the grand tapestry of the universe, there exists a force that is both powerful and tender, an energy that permeates every aspect of our lives. It is the force of motherhood, an embodiment of love, sacrifice and unwavering dedication. Mothers, fuelled by a mission to serve, are guided by the universal laws that govern their noble journey.

Here are seven universal laws that I believe are directly applicable for mothers.

LAW 1: THE LAW OF UNCONDITIONAL LOVE

At the very core of a mother's being lies an unyielding wellspring of unconditional love. It is a force that knows no bounds, surpassing space and time. A mother's love is steadfast, embracing her children in both their triumphs and their tribulations. It is a love that perseveres through challenges, nurturing and supporting, without expecting anything in return. This law reminds us that a mother's love is a divine gift, transcending all barriers.

LAW 2: THE LAW OF SACRIFICE

Motherhood is a path paved with selflessness and sacrifice. A mother willingly gives up her own desires, aspirations and sometimes even her dreams, in order to prioritise the wellbeing of her children. This law teaches us that true fulfilment comes not from personal gain but from the joy and happiness of those we hold dear. A mother's sacrifices are an enduring testament to her unwavering commitment to her children's growth and happiness.

LAW 3: THE LAW OF NURTURE

Mothers possess a unique ability to nurture, both physically and emotionally. They create an environment of safety, warmth and unconditional acceptance. Like a gardener tending to a delicate plant, a mother nurtures her children's minds, bodies and souls. This law teaches us that a mother's nurturing touch can foster strength, resilience and the seeds of greatness within her children.

LAW 4: THE LAW OF INTUITION

Mothers possess an innate wisdom and intuition that guides their actions. They can sense their children's needs, often before they are even expressed. This intuitive connection transcends rationality, tapping into a deeper realm of understanding. The law of intuition reminds us that a mother's instincts are a powerful tool, enabling her to provide guidance, support and protection, even in the face of uncertainty.

LAW 5: THE LAW OF BOUNDLESS ENERGY

Mothers seem to possess an infinite wellspring of energy, defying physical and emotional limitations. They tirelessly juggle multiple responsibilities, fulfilling their roles as nurturers, caregivers and providers. This law reminds us that a mother's energy comes not from external sources but from her unwavering love and dedication to her family. It is this boundless energy that propels her forward, enabling her to surmount any obstacle in her path.

LAW 6: THE LAW OF ENDLESS LEARNING

Motherhood is a journey of continuous growth and learning. As mothers navigate the ever-changing landscape of raising children, they acquire new knowledge, skills and perspectives. This law teaches us that a mother's willingness to embrace the unknown, to learn from her experiences and to adapt to new circumstances, is instrumental in her ability to serve her family with wisdom and grace.

LAW 7: THE LAW OF LEGACY

A mother's influence extends far beyond her immediate presence. Her love and teachings become ingrained in the hearts and minds of her children, leaving an indelible mark on future generations. This law reminds us that a mother's impact is everlasting, as her children carry forward her love, values and teachings, shaping the world with their own unique contributions.

In the vast expanse of the universe, mothers stand as radiant beacons of love, fuelled by an unwavering mission to serve. Guided by the universal laws of motherhood, mothers weave a tapestry of love, sacrifice and boundless devotion, leaving an enduring legacy that illuminates the path for generations to come. Embrace the profound significance of your role as a mother, for in doing so, you become a living embodiment of the universal laws, creating a ripple of love and transformation that reverberates throughout the cosmos. Trust in the power of your infinite well of love!

Life Magic Mastery
Master Gifts

I share my 7 master gifts with you in the hope that in you will benefit by guiding them to navigate the beautiful and sometimes challenging adventure of motherhood with grace and wisdom.

LIFE MAGIC MASTERY WITH MY 7 MASTER GIFTS

In the journey of life mastery, there are seven master gifts that I have lived through over the past three mothering decades, and I hope that by sharing them other moms can cultivate and embrace the magic of mindfulness, knowing, intention, love, gratitude, forgiveness and belief. Each of these gifts holds the power to transform your life and the lives of those around you.

Below I share the essence and beauty of these master gifts:

MINDFULNESS

By practicing mindfulness, moms develop a heightened awareness of the present moment, allowing them to savour the joys, navigate challenges and make conscious choices. Mindfulness enables them to be fully present and engage in meaningful connections with their children, nurturing deeper relationships and creating a sense of peace and balance within themselves.

KNOWING

Embracing their inner knowing, moms tap into their intuition and wisdom. This intuitive guidance helps them make decisions aligned with their values and desires, fostering clarity, confidence and a sense of purpose. Knowing empowers moms to trust themselves and their instincts, leading to a life filled with authenticity and alignment.

INTENTION

Setting powerful intentions empowers moms to consciously create the life they desire. By clarifying their goals and aligning their thoughts, emotions and actions with their intentions, they become deliberate creators of their reality. Intention gives moms the focus, determination and resilience needed to overcome obstacles and manifest their dreams.

LOVE

The law of love is a super fuel that moms can harness to infuse all aspects of their lives with compassion, kindness and empathy. By embodying love, moms cultivate nurturing relationships, foster emotional wellbeing, and create a harmonious environment for their children to thrive. Love becomes the guiding force that fuels their actions and creates a ripple effect of positive impact.

GRATITUDE

Gratitude serves as a life hack for busy moms to reconnect with the flow of manifesting. By shifting their perspective, cultivating a positive mindset and harnessing the power of vibrational energy, moms attract abundance and effortlessly manifest their desires. Gratitude becomes a daily practice that nurtures joy, contentment and a deep appreciation for life's blessings.

FORGIVENESS

Learning the art of forgiveness frees moms from the burden of past hurts and promotes emotional healing and growth. By forgiving themselves and others, moms create a nurturing environment for themselves and their children. Forgiveness strengthens relationships, fosters empathy and compassion and paves the way for a more virtuous and fulfilling life.

BELIEF

When moms believe in themselves as much as they believe in their children, they unlock their true potential. Self-belief inspires personal growth, resilience and the ability to create positive change. By recognising their worth, leading by example and embracing their authenticity, moms become powerful agents of transformation, radiating beauty and inspiring others to believe in themselves too.

These gifts have become pillars for me in all my choices and I have experienced firsthand the benefits of their mastery. I share them with you in the hope that in you will benefit by guiding them to navigate the beautiful and sometimes challenging adventure of motherhood with grace and wisdom.

Mindfulness

Mindfulness encourages moms to create moments of stillness and reflection, allowing them to recharge and regain clarity.

MOMS AND MINDFULNESS

Unlocking life's magic mastery

In the whirlwind of motherhood, finding moments of peace and stillness can seem like an elusive dream. However, the practice of mindfulness holds the key to unlocking the magic of mastery in a mother's life. By cultivating mindfulness, moms can tap into the present moment, embrace the beauty of each experience and navigate the journey of motherhood with grace and clarity.

THE POWER OF PRESENT-MOMENT AWARENESS

Mindfulness is the art of being fully present in the here and now, consciously engaging with each passing moment. For moms, who often juggle multiple tasks and responsibilities, mindfulness provides a sanctuary of calm amidst the chaos. By grounding themselves in the present, moms can savour the simple joys, fully experience their interactions with their children, and cultivate a deep sense of gratitude for the precious moments they share.

NURTURING SELF-COMPASSION AND ACCEPTANCE

Motherhood is a journey that brings both moments of triumph and challenges. Mindfulness allows moms to cultivate self-compassion and acceptance, embracing themselves fully, flaws and all. By acknowledging that imperfections are part of the human experience, moms can release the burden of self-judgement and approach their roles with kindness and understanding. This self-compassion becomes a nurturing force that flows to their children and creates an environment of love and acceptance.

EMBRACING THE POWER OF PAUSE

In the fast-paced world of motherhood, it is essential for moms to honour the power of pause. Mindfulness encourages moms to create moments of stillness and reflection, allowing them to recharge and regain clarity. By stepping back from the constant demands of their roles, moms can reconnect with their own needs, dreams and aspirations. The power of pause grants them the space to make conscious choices, set boundaries and align their actions with their values.

CULTIVATING MINDFUL CONNECTIONS

Moms are natural caregivers, but amidst their nurturing responsibilities, it is vital for them to cultivate mindful connections. Mindfulness enables moms to be fully present in their interactions with their children, partners and loved ones. By listening attentively, observing without judgement, and offering genuine empathy, moms foster deeper connections and create a loving and harmonious family dynamic. Mindful connections strengthen the bonds that fuel a mother's journey and enrich the lives of those she loves.

SAVOURING THE MAGIC OF EVERYDAY MOMENTS

Within the tapestry of motherhood, everyday moments hold extraordinary magic. Mindfulness invites moms to savour these moments fully, recognising their beauty and significance. Whether it is witnessing a child's laughter, embracing a tender hug or sharing a heartfelt conversation, mindfulness allows moms to drink deeply from life's precious moments. By immersing themselves in the present, moms create memories that resonate with love, joy and a profound sense of fulfilment.

NAVIGATING CHALLENGES WITH RESILIENCE

Motherhood presents its fair share of challenges, and mindfulness equips moms with the tools to navigate them with resilience and grace. By cultivating a non-judgemental awareness of their thoughts and emotions, moms can respond to difficulties from a place of calm and clarity. Mindfulness empowers them to pause, assess the situation and choose a mindful response rather than react impulsively. This resilience becomes a guiding light, illuminating the path through even the darkest of moments.

INTEGRATING MINDFULNESS INTO DAILY LIFE

Mindfulness is not limited to specific practices or dedicated moments of solitude. Moms can integrate mindfulness into their daily lives, infusing it into every aspect of their motherhood journey. By bringing mindful awareness to everyday tasks such as cooking, cleaning and playing with their children, moms transform routine activities into sacred rituals. They become attuned to the subtleties of their experiences, infusing them with presence and love. This practice promotes virtuous habits that will assist our children in becoming the best version of themselves in the future.

THE POWER OF MINDFULNESS

Cultivating presence in motherhood

Motherhood is a beautiful and transformative journey, filled with moments of joy, love and connection. Yet, it can also be overwhelming, with endless to-do lists, constant demands and the pressure to juggle multiple roles and responsibilities. In the midst of this whirlwind, it is easy to lose sight of the present moment and become caught up in worries about the future or regrets about the past. However, the power of mindfulness offers a transformative tool to bring us back to the present moment, allowing us to cultivate a deep sense of presence and find solace in the midst of chaos.

WHAT IS MINDFULNESS?

Mindfulness is the practice of deliberately bringing our attention to the present moment without judgement. It is about fully experiencing and being aware of what is happening in the here and now, without being consumed by thoughts of the past or future. In motherhood, mindfulness becomes a powerful tool that helps us navigate the challenges and joys of raising our children with a sense of calm, clarity and compassion.

THE GIFT OF PRESENCE

When we practice mindfulness in motherhood, we offer ourselves and our children the precious gift of presence. In a world filled with distractions and constant busyness, being fully present with our children becomes a profound act of love. By setting aside our worries, agendas and electronic devices, we create a sacred space for authentic connection and deep understanding. Our presence becomes a nurturing force, instilling in our children a sense of security, love and acceptance.

MINDFUL MOMENTS IN EVERYDAY LIFE

Mindfulness is not confined to formal meditation practice; it can be integrated into every aspect of our daily lives as mothers. From changing diapers to preparing meals, we can infuse mindfulness into these seemingly mundane tasks, transforming them into moments of presence and connection. By engaging our senses and fully immersing ourselves in the experience, we open ourselves to the richness of the present moment.

THE BREATH AS AN ANCHOR

The breath serves as a powerful anchor in cultivating mindfulness. It is always with us, readily accessible as a point of focus. By bringing our attention to the sensations of the breath, we ground ourselves in the present moment and cultivate a deep sense of calm. When we find ourselves feeling overwhelmed or scattered, taking a few conscious breaths can bring us back to the present, allowing us to respond to our children and life's challenges with greater clarity and compassion.

NAVIGATING EMOTIONS WITH MINDFULNESS

Motherhood can be an emotional roller-coaster, with moments of joy, frustration and everything in-between. Mindfulness offers a compassionate space to observe and navigate these emotions without being swept away by them. By cultivating an attitude of non-judgement and acceptance, we create a safe container for our emotions to arise and pass without clinging or aversion. Through mindfulness, we learn to respond to our emotions with kindness and wisdom, modelling emotional resilience for our children.

MINDFUL COMMUNICATION AND CONNECTION

Mindfulness also plays a vital role in our interactions with our children. By being fully present and attentive when they speak, we communicate that their thoughts and feelings matter. Mindful listening allows us to truly hear and understand our children, fostering open communication and deepening our connection with them. We also become more attuned to their non-verbal cues, picking up on their needs and desires with greater sensitivity.

FINDING STILLNESS IN CHAOS

Motherhood often feels like a whirlwind of activity, with a never-ending list of tasks and responsibilities. Yet, even in the midst of chaos, we can find moments of tranquility through mindfulness. Whether it's stealing a few minutes for a mindful cup of tea, a walk in nature or a brief meditation practice, these moments of pause and self-care replenish our energy and help us navigate the challenges of motherhood with grace and resilience.

CULTIVATING SELF-COMPASSION

Mindfulness invites us to cultivate self-compassion, acknowledging that we are doing our best as mothers and that it's okay to make mistakes.

Through mindful self-compassion practices, such as loving-kindness meditation and self-care rituals, we nurture ourselves and replenish our inner resources. By extending compassion to ourselves, we model self-love and acceptance to our children, empowering them to embrace their own imperfections and practice self-compassion.

EMBRACING THE JOURNEY

In conclusion, the power of mindfulness in motherhood lies in its ability to anchor us in the present moment, allowing us to fully experience the beauty and challenges of raising our children. Through the practice of mindfulness, we cultivate presence, deepen our connection with our children and find solace and inner calm amidst the chaos. As mothers, let us embrace this transformative tool and savour each precious moment of the journey with mindfulness and an open heart.

Cultivating a grateful mindset uplifts our energy and fosters a sense of contentment and wellbeing within our homes.

CONSCIOUS ENERGY

Nurturing a mindful presence as a mom

As moms, we hold a powerful influence over the energy within our homes and our relationships with our children. Our energy sets the tone for their emotional wellbeing and behaviour. By being mindful of our own energy and cultivating a positive and balanced state, we create a harmonious environment where our children can thrive. In this chapter, we explore the significance of conscious energy and how it impacts our role as moms.

THE POWER OF MINDFUL ENERGY

Our energy as moms is contagious. Children are highly attuned to the emotional atmosphere around them and often mirror the energy they perceive. By cultivating mindful energy, we become aware of our thoughts, emotions and the energetic vibration we emit. Mindful energy allows us to create a nurturing and supportive environment that positively influences our children's emotional state and overall wellbeing.

SELF-AWARENESS AND EMOTIONAL REGULATION

Self-awareness is a fundamental aspect of cultivating mindful energy. We become attuned to our own emotions, triggers and energy levels. By acknowledging and accepting our feelings, we can respond consciously rather than react impulsively. This self-awareness enables us to regulate our emotions, modelling healthy emotional management for our children. By practicing self-care and engaging in activities that replenish our energy, we can maintain a balanced state and show up as the calm and grounded presence our children need.

SETTING BOUNDARIES AND MODELLING HEALTHY RELATIONSHIPS

Mindful energy extends to setting boundaries and modelling healthy relationships. By setting clear and respectful boundaries with our children, we teach them the importance of self-care, personal space and mutual respect. We model healthy relationships by demonstrating effective communication, conflict resolution and empathy. Through these actions, we foster an environment where our children feel secure, respected and valued.

INTENTIONAL COMMUNICATION

Conscious energy is reflected in our communication with our children. We choose our words carefully, using language that is supportive, uplifting and encouraging. We actively listen to our children, offering them our undivided attention and validating their experiences. By practicing intentional communication, we cultivate an atmosphere of trust, openness and understanding.

PRACTICING PRESENCE

Being fully present with our children is a transformative practice. Mindful energy requires us to focus our attention on the present moment, giving our children the gift of our undivided presence. We engage in quality interactions, actively participating in their lives and cherishing the time spent together. By practicing presence, we deepen our connection with our children and create meaningful memories.

CULTIVATING GRATITUDE

Gratitude is a powerful tool for cultivating mindful energy. By practicing gratitude, we shift our focus to the positive aspects of our lives and the blessings within our family. We teach our children to appreciate the present moment and express gratitude for the simple joys in life. Cultivating a grateful mindset uplifts our energy and fosters a sense of contentment and wellbeing within our homes.

EMBRACING FLEXIBILITY AND ADAPTABILITY

Mindful energy involves embracing flexibility and adaptability. As moms, we navigate the ever-changing landscape of parenthood, and our ability to adapt to new circumstances influences our children's experience. By remaining open-minded and adaptable, we teach our children the value of resilience, problem-solving and embracing change. We model the ability to navigate challenges with grace and flexibility.

SELF-COMPASSION AND SELF-LOVE

Mindful energy includes practicing self-compassion and self-love. We recognise that we are imperfect beings, and it is okay to prioritise self-care and personal growth. By nurturing ourselves and filling our own cups, we replenish our energy reserves and show our children the importance of self-compassion. When we love and care for ourselves, we can show up as the best version of ourselves for our children.

Mindful parenting is rooted in the practice of mindfulness, which involves non-judgemental awareness of the present moment.

MINDFUL PARENTING

Nurturing conscious connections with your children

Parenting is a sacred journey that presents us with countless opportunities to connect deeply with our children, nurture their growth and create meaningful relationships. Mindful parenting is an approach that brings conscious awareness and presence to our interactions, allowing us to cultivate deeper connections and foster a nurturing environment for our children. In this chapter, we explore the principles and practices of mindful parenting and how they can enhance our relationship with our children, promoting their wellbeing and our own personal growth.

THE ESSENCE OF MINDFUL PARENTING

Mindful parenting is rooted in the practice of mindfulness, which involves non-judgemental awareness of the present moment. It invites us to bring our full attention and intention to the interactions we have with our children. By being fully present, we can listen with openness, respond with empathy and connect with our children on a deeper level.

Mindful parenting encourages us to embrace each moment as an opportunity for growth, connection and learning.

CULTIVATING PRESENCE AND AWARENESS

The foundation of mindful parenting lies in cultivating our own presence and awareness. We can develop a daily mindfulness practice that allows us to connect with ourselves, centre our attention and cultivate a sense of calm and clarity. By taking moments of stillness and self-reflection, we become more attuned to our own thoughts, emotions and triggers. This self-awareness helps us respond to our children from a place of conscious choice rather than reacting based on unconscious patterns.

LISTENING WITH COMPASSION

Mindful parenting involves active and compassionate listening. It means giving our children our full attention, putting aside distractions and truly hearing what they are saying, both verbally and non-verbally. By listening with empathy and an open heart, we validate their experiences, emotions and perspectives. This deepens the connection between parent and child, creating a safe space for them to express themselves authentically and fostering a sense of trust and understanding.

RESPONDING, NOT REACTING

Mindful parenting invites us to pause and reflect before responding to our children's behaviours or emotions. Rather than reacting impulsively out of frustration or anger, we can consciously choose our words and actions with intention and love. By responding instead of reacting, we model emotional regulation and teach our children the importance of thoughtful communication and problem-solving. This approach cultivates a sense of mutual respect and strengthens our connection with them.

CREATING RITUALS OF CONNECTION

Mindful parenting involves the creation of rituals and routines that foster connection and presence in our daily lives. This may include bedtime rituals, family meals or shared activities where we can engage with our children in a focused and meaningful way. These rituals provide opportunities for quality time, open communication and the expression of love and appreciation. They become anchors in our children's lives, nurturing their sense of security and deepening the bond between parent and child.

SELF-CARE AND SELF-COMPASSION

Mindful parenting recognises the importance of self-care and self-compassion. It reminds us that we cannot pour from an empty cup. Taking care of ourselves physically, emotionally and mentally allows us to show up fully for our children. By prioritising self-care, we model healthy habits and self-love, teaching our children the value of nurturing their own wellbeing. Self-compassion reminds us that parenting is a journey of learning, and it is okay to make mistakes. It invites us to be gentle with ourselves, practicing self-forgiveness and embracing personal growth along the way.

Mindful parenting is a powerful practice that allows us to nurture conscious connections with our children. By cultivating presence, listening with compassion, responding thoughtfully, creating rituals of connection, prioritising self-care and practicing self-compassion, we deepen our relationships with our children and foster an environment of love, understanding and growth. Mindful parenting invites us to savour the precious moments of parenthood, appreciating the journey as an opportunity for mutual learning and transformation. Let us embrace the power of mindfulness and consciously nurture our connections with our children, sowing the seeds of love and resilience that will flourish throughout their lives.

Recognise that taking care of yourself is not selfish but essential for your overall happiness and ability to be present for your children.

MINDFUL SELF-CARE

Nurturing your wellbeing as a mom

Motherhood is a beautiful journey filled with love, joy and countless responsibilities. In the midst of caring for our children and tending to their needs, it's crucial that we prioritise our own wellbeing. Self-care is not a luxury but a necessity, as it allows us to recharge, replenish our energy and show up as the best version of ourselves for our families. In this chapter, we explore the importance of mindful self-care and provide practical strategies for nurturing your wellbeing as a mom.

UNDERSTANDING THE ESSENCE OF SELF-CARE

Redefining self-care: Embrace the concept of self-care as a holistic practice that encompasses nurturing your physical, mental and emotional wellbeing. Recognise that taking care of yourself is not selfish but essential for your overall happiness and ability to be present for your children.

THE POWER OF MINDFUL SELF-CARE

Cultivating self-awareness: Develop a deeper understanding of your own needs, desires and limits. Practice mindfulness to tune into your emotions, thoughts and physical sensations, allowing yourself to respond with compassion and kindness.

Carving out intentional moments: Create intentional pockets of time for self-care throughout your day. It can be as simple as savouring a cup of tea, engaging in a hobby or practicing deep breathing exercises. Prioritise these moments and approach them with a sense of presence and gratitude.

NURTURING YOUR PHYSICAL WELLBEING

Prioritising rest and sleep: Recognise the importance of adequate rest and sleep for your overall wellbeing. Establish a bedtime routine that promotes relaxation and quality sleep, ensuring you wake up refreshed and energised.

Engaging in nourishing movement: Find joy in physical activity that suits your preferences and schedule. Whether it's a gentle yoga practice, a brisk walk in nature or dancing around the living room with your children, prioritise movement that energises and nourishes your body.

CARING FOR YOUR EMOTIONAL AND MENTAL WELLBEING

Honouring your emotions: Allow yourself to feel and express a wide range of emotions without judgement. Create a safe space for emotional release through journalling, talking with trusted friends or seeking professional support when needed.

Practicing mindfulness and meditation: Incorporate mindfulness and meditation practices into your daily routine. Cultivate moments of stillness, observe your thoughts without attachment and cultivate a sense of calm and clarity amidst the busyness of motherhood.

CREATING A SUPPORTIVE ENVIRONMENT

Seeking and accepting help: Recognise that asking for help is not a sign of weakness but a demonstration of self-awareness and strength. Reach out to family, friends or support groups to share responsibilities, offer guidance or provide much-needed breaks.

Establishing boundaries: Set healthy boundaries to protect your time, energy and emotional wellbeing. Learn to say no to commitments that do not align with your priorities and create space for activities and relationships that bring you joy and fulfilment.

CULTIVATING INNER CONNECTION AND FULFILMENT

Nurturing your passions and hobbies: Carve out time to engage in activities that bring you joy, fulfilment and a sense of purpose outside of motherhood. Explore your passions, develop new skills or reignite old hobbies that ignite your inner fire.

Cultivating gratitude and self-compassion: Practice gratitude for the blessings in your life, including the gift of motherhood. Foster self-compassion by treating yourself with kindness, embracing imperfections and celebrating your achievements, no matter how small.

Mindful self-care is an essential aspect of motherhood that allows us to nurture our wellbeing, cultivate inner balance and show up as the best versions of ourselves for our children. By prioritising self-care, we not only fill our own cups but also create a positive ripple effect in our families and communities. Embrace the power of mindful self-care and let it be a guiding force that supports you on your transformative journey of motherhood.

As moms awaken their perspective power through mindfulness, they unlock the full potential of their role, nurturing not only their children but also their own wellbeing and fulfilment.

PERSPECTIVE POWER FOR MOMS

Harnessing the superpower of mindfulness

In the fast-paced and demanding world of motherhood, it's easy for moms to get caught up in the whirlwind of responsibilities, tasks and the constant needs of their children. Amidst the chaos, it is essential for mothers to tap into their innate superpower: mindfulness. Mindfulness is a profound gift that allows moms to cultivate presence, find inner calm and gain a fresh perspective on the beautiful journey of motherhood.

In this chapter, we explore the transformative power of mindfulness as a tool for moms to navigate the ups and downs of their daily lives with grace and clarity. We dive into the depths of this ancient practice, uncovering its profound benefits and practical applications in the realm of motherhood. By embracing mindfulness, moms can tap into their life magic mastery, fostering a deep sense of connection, self-awareness and harmony within themselves and their families.

THE ESSENCE OF MINDFULNESS

Mindfulness is the art of paying attention to the present moment with intention, non-judgement and acceptance. It involves being fully present, aware of our thoughts, emotions and sensations, without getting lost in the past or consumed by worries about the future. By cultivating mindfulness, moms can anchor themselves in the richness of the present, savouring the small miracles and joys that unfold within their motherhood journey.

THE BENEFITS OF MINDFULNESS FOR MOMS

Cultivating inner calm: Motherhood can be overwhelming, filled with demands and responsibilities that can lead to stress and anxiety. Mindfulness offers a sanctuary of calm amidst the chaos, allowing moms to find inner peace, reduce stress and approach challenges with a clear and centred mind.

Deepening connection: Mindfulness enables moms to develop a deeper connection with their children by truly seeing them in each moment. By being fully present with their little ones, moms can engage in meaningful interactions, fostering trust and nurturing a strong bond of love.

Emotional regulation: The practice of mindfulness empowers moms to observe their emotions without judgement or reactivity. By cultivating emotional awareness and regulation, moms can respond to their children's needs with compassion and understanding, modelling healthy emotional expression and creating a harmonious environment.

Self-care and wellbeing: Mindfulness encourages moms to prioritise self-care and wellbeing. By carving out moments of stillness and self-reflection, moms can replenish their energy, cultivate self-compassion and meet their own needs, enabling them to show up as their best selves for their families.

Enhanced problem-solving: Mindfulness expands moms' capacity to approach challenges and solve problems with clarity and creativity. By embracing a non-judgemental mindset and observing situations from a fresh perspective, moms can tap into their innate wisdom and find innovative solutions to everyday issues.

PRACTICAL APPLICATIONS OF MINDFULNESS IN MOTHERHOOD

Mindful breathing: Taking a few conscious breaths throughout the day can serve as an anchor, bringing moms back to the present moment and calming their minds. A deep breath in, a slow exhale out and a moment of stillness can provide a reset and rejuvenation, allowing moms to approach their tasks with clarity and focus.

Daily mindful rituals: Infusing everyday activities with mindfulness can transform them into sacred rituals. From mindful feeding and bathing routines to bedtime rituals filled with presence and connection, moms can savour these moments, creating a sense of mindfulness and intention in their interactions with their children.

Mindful moments of self-care: Carving out time for self-care is crucial for moms, and infusing these moments with mindfulness magnifies their impact. Whether it's enjoying a cup of tea in solitude, taking a nature walk or engaging in a creative hobby, moms can bring mindfulness to these activities, nurturing their own wellbeing and replenishing their spirits.

Mindful parenting reflections: Setting aside dedicated time for reflection and introspection allows moms to deepen their self-awareness as parents. Journalling, guided meditation or simply sitting quietly and contemplating their parenting journey can help moms gain insights, identify patterns and make conscious choices aligned with their values and intentions.

Mindfulness is a transformative superpower that empowers moms to navigate the magical journey of motherhood with presence, grace and a fresh perspective. By harnessing the essence of mindfulness, moms can tap into their life magic mastery, fostering deeper connections, cultivating inner calm and embracing the joys and challenges of raising children with grace and gratitude. As moms awaken their perspective power through mindfulness, they unlock the full potential of their role, nurturing not only their children but also their own wellbeing and fulfilment.

Embracing the magic of mindful moments allows us to infuse our everyday lives with presence, awareness and deep appreciation.

THE MAGIC OF MINDFUL MOMENTS

Cultivating presence in everyday life

In the busyness and chaos of motherhood, it's easy to get caught up in the constant to-do lists, responsibilities and distractions. However, there is a profound beauty in slowing down, becoming present and fully engaging in each moment. In this chapter, we explore the magic of mindful moments and the transformative power they hold in cultivating presence and enhancing our experience as mothers. By embracing mindfulness in our everyday lives, we can create a deeper connection with ourselves, our children and the world around us.

THE ESSENCE OF MINDFULNESS

Understanding mindfulness: Gain an understanding of what mindfulness truly means. It is the practice of bringing our attention fully to the present moment, with non-judgemental awareness. It allows us to be fully present and engaged in the here and now, rather than being lost in regrets about the past or worries about the future.

Cultivating awareness: Develop a heightened sense of awareness of your thoughts, emotions and physical sensations. Notice the patterns and habits of your mind, and become more attuned to the present moment. Mindfulness helps us break free from autopilot and create space for conscious choices and responses.

Embracing non-judgement: Approach each moment with an attitude of non-judgement and acceptance. Release the need to label experiences as good or bad, right or wrong. Instead, cultivate an open-hearted curiosity and embrace whatever arises with kindness and compassion.

BRINGING MINDFULNESS TO EVERYDAY LIFE

Mindful moments with your children: Discover the magic of being fully present with your children. Engage in activities with a sense of mindfulness, such as playing, reading or simply having a conversation. Let go of distractions and give your full attention to the precious moments you share with them.

Mindful self-care: Incorporate mindfulness into your self-care routines. Whether it's taking a mindful walk, enjoying a soothing bath or savouring a cup of tea, engage in these activities with a sense of presence and gratitude. Use these moments to recharge and nourish yourself.

Mindful household tasks: Transform mundane chores into mindful rituals. Whether you're washing dishes, folding laundry or tidying up, bring your full attention to the task at hand. Notice the sensations, scents and movements involved, and approach each task as an opportunity for presence and mindfulness.

PRACTICAL TECHNIQUES FOR CULTIVATING MINDFUL MOMENTS

Breath awareness: Practice conscious breathing throughout the day. Take moments to pause, close your eyes if possible and bring your attention to your breath. Notice the sensations of inhalation and exhalation, allowing your breath to anchor you in the present moment.

Body scan meditation: Engage in a body scan meditation to tune into the sensations in your body. Starting from your toes and working your way up to the top of your head, bring gentle awareness to each part of your body, releasing tension and embracing the present moment.

Mindful pauses: Incorporate mindful pauses into your daily routine. These are short moments of stillness and presence where you pause whatever you're doing, take a few deep breaths and bring your attention back to the present moment.

Embracing the magic of mindful moments allows us to infuse our everyday lives with presence, awareness and deep appreciation. By cultivating mindfulness, we create a foundation of inner peace, joy and connection that ripples through our experiences as mothers. Mindful moments help us break free from the grip of busyness and cultivate a deep sense of gratitude for the beauty and wonder present in each moment. Embrace the magic of mindfulness and allow it to transform your experience as a mother, enabling you to savor the richness of life and create lasting memories with your children.

Knowing

When moms learn to embrace and trust their innate intuition, they unlock a profound source of guidance and empowerment, shaping their journey with authenticity, purpose and love.

EMBRACING INNER KNOWING

The path to success and heart-led motherhood

Within every mother resides a deep well of wisdom, an inner knowing that holds the key to both personal success and heart-led motherhood. When moms learn to embrace and trust their innate intuition, they unlock a profound source of guidance and empowerment, shaping their journey with authenticity, purpose and love.

UNLEASHING THE POWER OF INTUITION

Intuition is the language of the soul, a subtle whisper that guides moms on their path. When moms learn to tune in and trust their intuition, they tap into a wellspring of wisdom that transcends logic and reasoning. Intuition becomes their compass, guiding them in making decisions that align with their values, passions and the wellbeing of their families. By embracing their inner knowing, moms step into their power, embracing the fullness of their unique capabilities.

FINDING AUTHENTICITY AND PURPOSE

Embracing inner knowing allows moms to uncover their authentic selves and live in alignment with their true purpose. When they listen to their intuition, moms are guided to make choices that honour their values, passions and desires. They shed societal expectations and embrace their own unique journey, fostering a deep sense of fulfilment and contentment. Through inner knowing, moms discover their purpose and their actions become heart-led and purpose-driven.

NURTURING HEART-LED MOTHERHOOD

Heart-led motherhood is a transformative approach that places love, compassion and connection at the core of maternal relationships. When moms embrace their inner knowing, they connect with the inherent wisdom that lies within their hearts. They lead with empathy, kindness and understanding, fostering deep bonds with their children. Heart-led motherhood embraces conscious parenting, mindful communication and nurturing environments, where love and respect are foundational.

CULTIVATING TRUST AND SELF-CONFIDENCE

Embracing inner knowing nurtures trust in oneself and fosters self-confidence. Moms who trust their intuition believe in their ability to make wise decisions and navigate the challenges of motherhood. As they lean into their inner knowing, they cultivate a deep sense of self-assurance, recognising that they possess the innate wisdom to guide their children's growth and wellbeing. Trusting their intuition empowers moms to step into leadership roles, both within their families and in their broader communities.

CREATING A SUPPORTIVE COMMUNITY

Moms who embrace their inner knowing understand the power of surrounding themselves with a supportive community. They seek like-minded individuals who value intuition and heart-led living. In these communities, moms find encouragement, inspiration and validation for their unique journeys. They engage in meaningful conversations, share experiences and uplift one another, fostering an environment that nurtures personal growth and collective wisdom.

BALANCING INTUITION AND PRACTICALITY

Embracing inner knowing does not negate the importance of practicality and planning. Rather, it harmonises intuition with the realities of daily life. Moms who trust their inner knowing strike a balance between intuition and practicality, using their innate wisdom to make informed decisions while considering the practical aspects of their choices. They blend the magic of intuition with the pragmatism needed to navigate the complexities of motherhood.

CONTINUAL GROWTH AND LEARNING

Embracing inner knowing is a lifelong journey of growth and learning. Moms who trust their intuition understand that they are always evolving and expanding their understanding. They seek opportunities for personal development, engaging in self-reflection and embracing new knowledge. They remain open to growth, recognising that their inner knowing evolves alongside their own growth as mothers and individuals.

As moms learn to embrace their inner knowing, they unlock the gateway to success and heart-led motherhood. Trusting their intuition, they navigate the journey of motherhood with authenticity, purpose and love. Through inner knowing, they become powerful agents of positive change, shaping their lives

EMBRACING KNOWING

Trusting your intuition as a mom

Motherhood is a journey filled with countless decisions, big and small. From the moment we hold our newborn in our arms, we are faced with choices that shape the lives of our children and ourselves. In a world filled with information, opinions and external pressures, it can be challenging to discern the best path forward. However, deep within us lies a profound source of wisdom – our intuition. In this chapter, we explore the power of embracing knowing and trusting our intuition as mothers.

THE VOICE WITHIN

Intuition is often described as a quiet, inner voice that guides us towards what feels right and aligned with our deepest values and desires. As mothers, we have a unique connection to this intuitive knowing. Our bond with our children opens us to a heightened sensitivity, allowing us to tap into our intuition and make decisions that serve their highest good. By learning to listen and trust this inner voice, we can navigate the complexities of motherhood with greater clarity and confidence.

CULTIVATING TRUST IN YOUR INTUITION

Trusting our intuition requires us to cultivate a deep sense of self-trust and self-belief. It involves letting go of the need for external validation and embracing the wisdom that resides within us. By honouring our intuition, we validate our own experiences and choices as mothers. This trust grows stronger with practice, as we learn to distinguish between the voice of fear or societal expectations and the gentle, knowing whispers of our intuition.

RECOGNISING THE SIGNS

Intuition speaks to us in various ways. It may manifest as a gut feeling, a sudden knowing, or a sense of resonance or discomfort. As mothers, we can learn to recognise the signs and signals that our intuition provides. It may be a sensation in the pit of our stomach when something feels off or a deep sense of peace and assurance when we are on the right path. By paying attention to these subtle cues, we become more attuned to our intuition's guidance.

QUIETENING THE MIND

In our fast-paced, information-driven world, it can be challenging to hear the whispers of our intuition amidst the noise. Cultivating practices that quieten the mind, such as meditation, mindfulness or journalling, can create space for our intuitive wisdom to emerge. By intentionally creating moments of stillness and silence, we create a fertile ground for our intuition to speak and guide us.

NURTURING INTUITION THROUGH SELF-CARE

Self-care plays a crucial role in nurturing our intuition. When we prioritise self-care, we replenish our energy and create a sense of inner calm. This state of wellbeing allows us to access our intuition more readily. Engaging in activities that nourish our mind, body and spirit, such as spending time in nature, practicing yoga or engaging in creative pursuits, nurtures our intuitive knowing and strengthens our connection to ourselves and our children.

NAVIGATING THE NOISE

As mothers, we often face a barrage of conflicting advice and opinions from well-meaning friends, family and societal norms. While it's essential to gather information and seek support, it's equally important to discern what resonates with our intuition and aligns with our values. By filtering out the noise and tuning into our inner guidance, we can make decisions that are in harmony with our authentic selves and the unique needs of our children.

HONOURING YOUR MOTHER'S INTUITION

Mother's intuition is a gift that we possess inherently. It is a wisdom that has been passed down through generations of mothers who have nurtured and protected their children. By honouring our own intuition, we acknowledge the wisdom of our ancestors and become part of this lineage. Trusting our intuition allows us to tap into this collective wisdom and make choices that are grounded in love, understanding and the deepest knowing of what is best for our children.

In conclusion, embracing knowing and trusting our intuition as mothers empowers us to navigate the complexities of motherhood with grace and confidence. By quietening the external noise, cultivating self-trust and nurturing our intuitive connection, we access a wellspring of wisdom that guides us in making decisions aligned with our values and the highest good of our children. Let us embrace our intuitive knowing and honour the profound wisdom that resides within us as mothers.

As mothers, cultivating our inner knowing allows us to tap into a wellspring of wisdom that goes beyond external advice or societal expectations.

THE WISDOM OF KNOWING

Making decisions aligned with your truth

Motherhood is filled with countless decisions, both big and small, that shape the lives of our children and ourselves. In the midst of the noise and opinions that surround us, it is crucial to tap into our inner wisdom and make decisions that align with our truth. This chapter explores the importance of knowing, trusting and honouring our intuition as mothers, empowering us to make choices that reflect our values, nurture our children's wellbeing and honour our own growth and authenticity.

CULTIVATING INNER KNOWING

Inner knowing, also known as intuition, is a deep sense of inner guidance and wisdom that resides within each of us. It is a subtle, yet powerful, voice that speaks to us when we listen closely. As mothers, cultivating our inner knowing allows us to tap into a wellspring of wisdom that goes beyond external advice or societal expectations. By connecting with our intuition, we can make decisions that are aligned with our deepest values, desires and truths.

LISTENING TO THE WHISPERS OF INTUITION

Intuition often speaks to us through whispers – subtle nudges, gut feelings or a sense of clarity that arises from within. To truly listen to our intuition, we must create space for stillness and reflection in our lives. This may involve practices such as meditation, journalling or simply taking moments of solitude to tune in and listen to the wisdom that emerges. By honouring these whispers, we can make decisions that resonate with our hearts and lead us towards greater fulfilment and purpose.

NAVIGATING EXTERNAL INFLUENCES

In a world filled with external influences and opinions, it can be challenging to stay true to our own knowing. Society, family and well-meaning friends may offer advice or expectations that conflict with our inner truth. In these moments, it is crucial to cultivate discernment and differentiate between external voices and our own intuitive guidance. By recognising that we are the experts of our own lives and our children's wellbeing, we can confidently make decisions that align with our values and aspirations.

TRUSTING YOUR INSTINCTS

Trusting our instincts as mothers is a vital aspect of honouring our inner knowing. Our instincts are a culmination of our life experiences, wisdom and the deep connection we share with our children. By trusting ourselves and the innate bond we have with our children, we can navigate the complexities of motherhood with confidence. Trusting our instincts allows us to make decisions from a place of authenticity and love, fostering an environment of trust and security for our children.

HONOURING YOUR AUTHENTICITY

Motherhood can sometimes tempt us to conform to societal norms or compare ourselves to others. However, true fulfilment and growth come from honouring our authentic selves. When we make decisions aligned with our truth, we model authenticity to our children, empowering them to embrace their own uniqueness and live authentically. By honouring our authenticity, we create a nurturing space for our children to explore their own identities and dreams.

EMBRACING GROWTH AND EVOLUTION

As we cultivate our inner knowing and make decisions aligned with our truth, we must also embrace the reality that our truth may evolve and change over time. Motherhood is a journey of growth and trans-formation, and as we learn and evolve, our decisions may naturally shift along with us. By staying open to growth and embracing the journey of self-discovery, we create a dynamic and empowering environment for ourselves and our children.

The wisdom of knowing empowers us as mothers to make decisions that align with our truth and nurture the wellbeing of our children. By cultivating our inner knowing, listening to the whispers of intuition, navigating external influences with discernment, trusting our instincts, honouring our authenticity and embracing growth and evolution, we become conscious decision-makers and role models for our children. Let us embrace the wisdom of knowing and navigate the beautiful journey of motherhood with confidence and grace.

By aligning your choices with your intuition, you can approach motherhood with confidence and clarity.

UNLEASHING YOUR INNER KNOWING

Tapping into intuition for guidance and wisdom

As mothers, we are often faced with countless decisions and choices on a daily basis. Amidst the noise and external influences, there is a powerful source of wisdom within us – our intuition. In this chapter, we explore the importance of tapping into our inner knowing and harnessing the guidance and wisdom it offers. By connecting with our intuition, we can navigate motherhood with clarity, confidence and a deep sense of alignment with our true selves.

THE POWER OF INTUITION

Understanding intuition: Intuition is a subtle, yet powerful, inner voice that guides us from within. It is a deep knowing that arises beyond logic and reasoning. Intuition speaks to us through feelings, gut instincts and subtle cues, offering insights and guidance that may not be immediately apparent.

Honouring your inner voice: Recognise the importance of listening to and honouring your inner voice. Often, we second-guess ourselves or seek external validation, disregarding our intuition. By cultivating trust and respect for our inner knowing, we can tap into a wellspring of wisdom and make decisions that are aligned with our highest good and the wellbeing of our children.

CULTIVATING A STRONG CONNECTION WITH INTUITION

Creating space for stillness: Set aside regular time for quiet reflection and stillness. This could be through meditation, journalling or simply finding moments of solitude. By creating space for stillness, we allow our intuition to rise to the surface and be heard.

Trusting your instincts: Practice trusting your instincts and acting upon them. Start with small decisions and observe the outcomes. As you witness the positive results of following your intuition, your trust in its guidance will grow.

Noticing subtle cues: Pay attention to the subtle cues and signals that arise within you. These can be physical sensations, emotions or intuitive nudges. Train yourself to notice and interpret these cues, as they often carry valuable insights and wisdom.

NAVIGATING MOTHERHOOD WITH INTUITION

Parenting from the heart: Let your intuition guide your parenting decisions and actions. When faced with challenging situations, tune in to your inner knowing and respond with love, compassion and wisdom. Trust that your intuition will lead you to make choices that best serve your children's growth and wellbeing.

Making decisions with confidence: When confronted with important decisions, consult your intuition as a trusted advisor. Tap into the deep well of wisdom within you and trust that the answers will come.

By aligning your choices with your intuition, you can approach motherhood with confidence and clarity.

Embracing flexibility and adaptability: Intuition often guides us to be flexible and adaptable in our approach to motherhood. Embrace the wisdom of your inner knowing as it prompts you to let go of rigid expectations and flow with the ever-changing nature of parenting.

NURTURING YOUR INTUITION

Self-care and intuition: Engage in self-care practices that nourish your mind, body and spirit. When you prioritise self-care, you create a fertile ground for your intuition to thrive. Make time for activities that bring you joy, inspire creativity and connect you with your inner self.

Surrounding yourself with support: Seek out like-minded individuals who value intuition and support your journey of tapping into your inner knowing. Surround yourself with people who uplift and inspire you, and with whom you can share experiences and insights.

Unleashing your inner knowing and tapping into your intuition is a profound gift that enhances your experience of motherhood. By honouring and trusting this deep well of wisdom, you can navigate the complexities of parenting with grace, confidence and authenticity. As you cultivate a strong connection with your intuition, you will find that your decisions align more harmoniously with your values, your children's needs and your own personal growth. Embrace the power of your inner knowing, and allow it to guide you on the beautiful journey of motherhood.

Intention

When moms set focused intentions, they tap into the limitless potential of the universe.

THE POWER OF FOCUSED INTENTIONS

Creating miracles in motherhood and beyond

Within every mother lies the potential to create miracles, to manifest profound transformations in their own lives and the lives of others. By harnessing the power of focused intentions, moms can unleash a force of manifestation that brings forth extraordinary outcomes and creates a ripple effect of positive change.

UNDERSTANDING THE POWER OF INTENTIONS

Intentions are the seeds of creation, the conscious desires and aspirations that shape our reality. When moms set focused intentions, they tap into the limitless potential of the universe. By clarifying their intentions and aligning them with their values and highest good, moms become co-creators of their own destinies. They unleash a powerful force that propels them forward on their journey of motherhood and empowers them to make a profound impact on the world around them.

CULTIVATING CLARITY AND FOCUS

Focused intentions require clarity and focus. Moms who cultivate a clear vision of their desires and goals can direct their energy and attention toward manifesting them. By becoming intentional in their thoughts, words and actions, moms align their entire being with their chosen path. Clarity and focus act as a beacon, guiding them through the complexities of motherhood and illuminating the steps needed to manifest their intentions.

ALIGNING WITH THE LAW OF ATTRACTION

The law of attraction states that like attracts like, and moms can harness this universal law to create miracles in their lives. By embodying the qualities and vibrations of their intentions, moms draw in the circumstances, opportunities and resources needed to manifest their desires. They cultivate a positive mindset, gratitude and unwavering belief in the fulfilment of their intentions. As they align with the law of attraction, moms magnetise miracles into their lives and the lives of those they love.

EMBRACING CO-CREATION AND COLLABORATION

Moms who set powerful intentions understand that they are co-creators with the universe. They recognise that they do not walk their motherhood journey alone but are supported by unseen forces and interconnected energies. By embracing the concept of co-creation, moms open themselves to collaboration with the universe, allowing synchronicities and divine guidance to guide them. They surrender the need for control and trust in the unfolding of miracles, knowing that they are supported every step of the way.

PRACTICING MINDFULNESS AND VISUALISATION

Mindfulness and visualisation are potent tools that support the manifestation of focused intentions. By practicing mindfulness, moms become fully present in the moment, attuned to the subtle cues and opportunities that arise. They cultivate a deep connection with their inner knowing and intuition, which guides them towards the actions needed to manifest their intentions. Visualisation amplifies the power of intentions, as moms vividly imagine and feel themselves living their desired reality. Through these practices, moms tap into the realm of possibilities and ignite the creative forces within.

TAKING INSPIRED ACTION

Focused intentions are not mere wishes; they require inspired action. Moms who are committed to manifesting their intentions take courageous steps towards their goals. They seize opportunities, overcome challenges and persistently move forward, fuelled by their unwavering belief in the miracles they are creating. By aligning their actions with their intentions, moms become catalysts for transformation, both in their own lives and in the lives of others.

EMBRACING GRATITUDE AND CELEBRATION

Gratitude and celebration are essential components of manifesting miracles. Moms who practice gratitude amplify their positive vibrations, attracting more blessings into their lives. They acknowledge and appreciate the progress they have made, celebrating even the smallest victories along the way. Gratitude and celebration create a magnetic field of abundance and joy, propelling moms forward on their journey of creating miracles.

As moms focus their intentions and tap into the power within, they become conduits for miracles in their lives.

Before setting intentions, it is essential to reflect on our values — those guiding principles that shape our choices and actions.

SETTING POWERFUL INTENTIONS

Manifesting your ideal motherhood journey

Motherhood is a journey of profound transformation and growth. As mothers, we have the incredible opportunity to shape not only the lives of our children but also our own experience of motherhood. Setting powerful intentions becomes a key tool in manifesting our ideal motherhood journey – a journey filled with love, joy, fulfilment and alignment with our deepest desires and values.

THE POWER OF INTENTION

Intention is the conscious and deliberate focus of our thoughts and desires. It is the driving force behind the manifestation of our dreams and aspirations. When we set powerful intentions, we harness the creative power of our minds to bring about the experiences we envision for ourselves and our families. Intention acts as a compass, guiding us towards the life we desire as mothers.

ALIGNING WITH YOUR VALUES

Before setting intentions, it is essential to reflect on our values – those guiding principles that shape our choices and actions. Our values serve as the foundation for our intentions, ensuring that they are rooted in authenticity and align with what truly matters to us. By identifying our core values, such as love, compassion, growth or balance, we can set intentions that reflect our deepest desires and lead to a more fulfilling motherhood experience.

CRAFTING YOUR IDEAL MOTHERHOOD VISION

To manifest our ideal motherhood journey, it is crucial to create a clear vision of what we desire. Take the time to envision your ideal motherhood experience – the type of relationship you want to have with your children, the values you want to instil in them, the quality of connection and communication you seek and the overall atmosphere and energy you want to cultivate in your home. This vision becomes the guiding light that shapes your intentions and directs your actions.

THE POWER OF AFFIRMATIONS

Affirmations are positive statements that reinforce our intentions and beliefs. By repeating affirmations daily, we reprogram our subconscious mind, aligning it with our conscious desires. As mothers, we can create affirmations that reflect our ideal motherhood experience. For example, 'I am a patient and loving mother,' 'I embrace the joy of motherhood every day,' or, 'I trust my instincts and make decisions that serve the highest good of my children.' Affirmations become powerful reminders of our intentions and help us stay focused on manifesting our desired reality.

PRACTICING VISUALISATION

Visualisation is a powerful tool that supports the manifestation process.

By vividly imagining ourselves living our ideal motherhood experience, we activate our subconscious mind and create a blueprint for manifestation. Take time each day to visualise yourself engaged in nurturing activities with your children, experiencing deep connections and embodying the qualities and values you desire as a mother. Feel the emotions associated with this vision and let them permeate your being.

TAKING INSPIRED ACTION

While intentions and visualisation are essential, they must be complemented by inspired action. Manifestation requires us to take intentional steps towards our goals and desires. As mothers, this may involve implementing new parenting strategies, seeking support or education, creating meaningful rituals and traditions or nurturing our own personal growth. When we align our actions with our intentions, we open ourselves up to opportunities and synchronicities that support our desired outcomes.

SURRENDERING AND TRUSTING THE PROCESS

As we set intentions and take inspired action, it is crucial to remember the importance of surrender and trust. Sometimes, the manifestation of our intentions may unfold differently than we expect. It is essential to release attachment to specific outcomes and trust that the universe is working in our favour. Surrendering allows us to embrace the flow of life and welcome unexpected gifts and opportunities that align with our deepest desires.

CELEBRATING AND REFLECTING

Throughout our motherhood journey, it is vital to celebrate our manifestations and reflect on our progress. Take time to acknowledge and appreciate the moments and experiences that align with your intentions. Reflect on the growth and lessons learned along the way. By celebrating and reflecting, we cultivate a mindset of gratitude and open ourselves up to even more manifestations and blessings.

In conclusion, setting powerful intentions is a transformative practice that empowers us to manifest our ideal motherhood journey. By aligning with our values, crafting a clear vision, using affirmations, practicing visualisation, taking inspired action, surrendering and celebrating, we become active co-creators of our motherhood experience. Let us embrace the power of intention and embark on a journey of conscious manifestation, creating a fulfilling and joyous motherhood experience for ourselves and our children.

Visualise the ideals and aspirations you have for your family as a whole.

INTENTIONAL PARENTING

Creating a vision and purpose for your family

Parenting is an incredible responsibility and opportunity to shape the lives of our children. Yet, it's easy to get caught up in the day-to-day challenges and lose sight of the bigger picture. In this chapter, we explore the power of intentional parenting and the importance of creating a vision and purpose for your family. By setting clear intentions and aligning your actions with your values, you can create a nurturing and meaningful environment that supports the growth and wellbeing of your entire family.

DEFINING YOUR FAMILY VISION

Reflecting on values: Take time to reflect on your core values and what matters most to you as a family. Consider aspects such as love, kindness, resilience, education, creativity or any other values that resonate with you. These values will serve as the foundation for your family vision.

Envisioning the future: Imagine the kind of family dynamic and atmosphere you wish to create. How do you want your children to feel within your family? What kind of relationships do you want to foster? Visualise the ideals and aspirations you have for your family as a whole.

SETTING INTENTIONAL GOALS

Identifying priorities: Determine the areas of focus that align with your family values and vision. This could include emotional wellbeing, education, character development, spirituality or any other aspects that are important to you. Identify specific goals within each area to guide your actions and choices as parents.

Collaborative goal-setting: Involve your partner and children, if appropriate, in the goal-setting process. Encourage open and honest communication to ensure that everyone's perspectives and desires are taken into consideration. This promotes a sense of ownership and commitment to the family's vision.

CREATING RITUALS AND PRACTICES

Daily rituals: Establish daily rituals that align with your family vision and support your goals. These could be morning routines, mealtime conversations, bedtime rituals or any other intentional practices that promote connection, growth and wellbeing.

Celebrations and traditions: Intentionally create family celebrations and traditions that reinforce your values and strengthen your bond. Whether it's a weekly family game night, an annual vacation or holiday traditions, these rituals serve as anchors and reminders of your family's purpose.

LIVING WITH INTENTION

Mindful decision-making: Practice making decisions in alignment with your family vision and goals. When faced with choices, ask yourself how each option supports or detracts from your desired outcomes. Let your intentions guide your actions and strive for consistency between your values and behaviours.

Modelling behaviour: Be mindful of the example you set for your children through your own actions and attitudes. Demonstrate the values and qualities you wish to instil in them. By embodying your family's vision, you inspire and empower your children to do the same.

FLEXIBILITY AND GROWTH

Embracing change: Recognise that your family's vision and goals may evolve over time. Be open to adjusting and adapting as your children grow and as circumstances change. Embrace flexibility while staying true to your core values and purpose.

Embracing imperfection: Parenting is a journey filled with ups and downs. Understand that you won't always get it right, and that's okay. Embrace the imperfections and learn from the challenges. Cultivate a mindset of growth and resilience, allowing room for mistakes and growth opportunities.

Intentional parenting is a transformative approach that empowers you to shape the experience of your family. By creating a vision and purpose, setting intentional goals and living in alignment with your values, you can cultivate a loving and nurturing environment where your children can thrive. Embrace the power of intention and let it guide you on the beautiful journey of parenting, knowing that your actions are purposeful and impactful in shaping the lives of your children.

Trusting that the universe supports our intentions

and that everything unfolds in divine timing

allows us to release attachment to specific outcomes

CREATING MIRACLES

Harnessing the power of intention in motherhood

As mothers, we possess an incredible power to manifest miracles in our lives and the lives of our children through the focused and intentional use of our energy and intentions. Intention is the conscious directing of our thoughts, emotions and actions towards a desired outcome. In this chapter, we explore the profound impact of harnessing the power of intention in motherhood and how it can create extraordinary experiences and transformations.

THE POWER OF INTENTION

Intention acts as a catalyst for manifestation, allowing us to align our thoughts, beliefs and actions with our deepest desires and dreams. When we set clear and powerful intentions, we tap into the infinite potential of the universe and invite miracles to unfold in our lives. Intention serves as a guiding force, directing our energy towards what we want to create and manifest for ourselves and our children.

CLARIFYING YOUR INTENTIONS

To harness the power of intention, it is essential to clarify what we truly desire for ourselves and our children. Reflecting on our values, aspirations and the kind of experiences we want to create allows us to set clear intentions. Whether it is fostering a loving and nurturing environment, supporting our children's growth and development, or manifesting specific goals, defining our intentions provides a road map for our actions and decisions as mothers.

ALIGNING WITH UNIVERSAL LAWS

Intention works in harmony with the universal laws that govern our reality. Understanding and aligning with these laws amplifies the power of our intentions. The law of attraction, for instance, states that like attracts like. By aligning our thoughts, emotions and actions with our intentions, we attract corresponding experiences and opportunities into our lives. The law of cause and effect reminds us that our intentions and actions have consequences, shaping our reality and the experiences of our children.

CULTIVATING A POSITIVE MINDSET

A positive and empowered mindset is essential for manifesting miracles through intention. By cultivating beliefs that support our intentions and focusing on positive possibilities, we create an energetic vibration that attracts favourable outcomes. Shifting from a mindset of limitation and doubt to one of possibility and abundance opens the doors to miraculous experiences in our lives and the lives of our children.

TAKING INSPIRED ACTION

Setting intentions is not enough; we must also take inspired action aligned with our intentions. Action serves as the bridge between our intentions and their manifestation. By taking small, consistent steps towards our desired outcomes, we demonstrate our commitment and dedication to realising our intentions. Inspired action can include seeking opportunities, making conscious choices and stepping out of our comfort zones to create the miracles we desire.

TRUSTING THE PROCESS

While setting intentions and taking action, it is crucial to trust the process and surrender to the divine flow of life. Trusting that the universe supports our intentions and that everything unfolds in divine timing allows us to release attachment to specific outcomes. This trust opens us to receive unexpected miracles and blessings that may surpass our initial intentions, bringing greater joy, growth and fulfilment into our lives.

CELEBRATING MANIFESTATIONS

As we witness our intentions manifesting in our lives and the lives of our children, it is essential to celebrate and express gratitude for these miracles. By acknowledging and appreciating the manifestations, we reinforce the power of intention and cultivate a sense of abundance and joy. Celebrating these miracles also inspires us to continue setting intentions and manifesting more magic in our motherhood journey.

Harnessing the power of intention in motherhood is a transformative practice that empowers us to create extraordinary experiences and miracles for ourselves and our children. By clarifying our intentions, aligning with universal laws, cultivating a positive mindset, taking inspired action, trusting the process and celebrating manifestations, we tap into the unlimited potential of our role as mothers. Let us embrace the power of intention and invite miracles to unfold in our lives, fostering a sense of wonder, fulfilment and magic in our journey of motherhood.

Love

*It empowers them to face the challenges and
demands of motherhood with grace and resilience.*

THE LAW OF LOVE

Super fuel for moms in all aspects of life

Love is a universal force that transcends boundaries, transforms lives and holds the power to propel moms to extraordinary heights in all aspects of their lives. By embracing the law of love, moms tap into a limitless wellspring of energy, compassion and resilience, fuelling their journey of motherhood and enriching every facet of their existence.

THE ESSENCE OF THE LAW OF LOVE

The law of love states that love is the fundamental essence of the universe, the cohesive force that unites all beings. Moms who embrace this law understand that love is not just an emotion but a way of being, a guiding principle that infuses every thought, word and action. By embodying love in all aspects of their lives, moms open themselves to the transformative power of this universal force.

LOVE AS A SOURCE OF STRENGTH

Love is a profound source of strength for moms. It empowers them to face the challenges and demands of motherhood with grace and resilience. When moms approach their roles from a place of love, they find the inner fortitude to weather the storms, overcome obstacles and rise above adversity. Love becomes an unwavering anchor, providing moms with the strength to navigate the complexities of their daily lives.

NURTURING SELF-LOVE AND SELF-CARE

The law of love reminds moms of the importance of nurturing self-love and practicing self-care. By prioritising their wellbeing and honouring their own needs, moms fill their own cup, ensuring they have an abundant reserve of love to give to their children and loved ones. Self-love and self-care become acts of empowerment, allowing moms to show up as their best selves and radiate love to those around them.

LOVE AS A GUIDE FOR DECISION-MAKING

Love serves as a compass for moms, guiding them in their decision-making process. When faced with choices, moms who embrace the law of love pause and ask themselves, *What would love do?* Love becomes the guiding light that illuminates the path of integrity, compassion and kindness. By making decisions from a place of love, moms create a ripple effect of positive impact in their families and communities.

CULTIVATING LOVE-FILLED RELATIONSHIPS

The law of love reminds moms of the importance of cultivating love-filled relationships. Moms who embody love in their interactions foster deep connections, open communication and emotional intimacy with their children, partners and loved ones. Love becomes the foundation on which trust, understanding and support are built. By nurturing love-filled relationships, moms create a harmonious and nurturing environment that fosters growth and happiness.

SPREADING LOVE AS A RIPPLE EFFECT

The love that moms embody extends beyond their immediate circles. It becomes a ripple effect that spreads far and wide, touching the lives of others. By radiating love, moms inspire and uplift those they encounter, creating a positive impact in their communities and beyond. Love becomes a transformative force that transcends boundaries, promoting unity, compassion and collective wellbeing.

LOVE AS A CATALYST FOR CHANGE

The law of love empowers moms to be catalysts for positive change in the world. By embodying love, moms become advocates for justice, equality and kindness. They stand up for what they believe in, using their voices and actions to create a more loving and inclusive society for their children and future generations. Love becomes a driving force that ignites their passion and fuels their mission to make a difference.

As moms embrace the law of love, they tap into a super fuel that propels them to extraordinary heights in all aspects of their lives. Love becomes the guiding principle that shapes their journey of motherhood, nurturing their own wellbeing, fostering deep connections and creating a ripple effect of positive change in the world.

We guide them as they navigate the complexities of life, always ready to offer guidance and support when needed.

GUIDING WITH LOVE

Embracing a supportive approach in motherhood

Motherhood is a remarkable journey filled with the responsibility of guiding our children. As moms, we are not meant to be controllers, but rather compassionate guides who support and empower our children to become the best versions of themselves. By embracing a nurturing and supportive approach, we create an environment that fosters growth, independence and mutual respect.

ENCOURAGING INDIVIDUALITY

Each child is a unique individual with their own dreams, talents and aspirations. As moms, we embrace and celebrate their individuality. We encourage them to explore their interests, express their thoughts and feelings and pursue their passions. By honouring their individuality, we inspire them to develop a strong sense of self and discover their own paths in life.

ACTIVE LISTENING

Effective guidance begins with active listening. We create space for our children to share their thoughts, concerns and experiences without judgement or interruption. By truly listening, we validate their feelings and perspectives, fostering trust and open communication. Through active listening, we gain insights into their needs and aspirations, allowing us to provide guidance that is tailored to their unique journeys.

OFFERING SUPPORT AND ENCOURAGEMENT

Our role as moms is to offer unwavering support and encouragement. We cheer our children on as they face challenges and celebrate their achievements, big and small. By acknowledging their efforts and providing reassurance, we nurture their self-esteem and confidence. Our support becomes a foundation from which they can explore, learn and grow.

TEACHING EMPATHY AND COMPASSION

Guiding our children involves teaching them essential values such as empathy and compassion. We model these qualities in our interactions with them and others. By cultivating empathy, we help them understand and respect the feelings and experiences of others. Through compassion, we teach them the importance of kindness, generosity and making a positive impact on the world around them.

NURTURING INDEPENDENCE

As moms, our goal is to nurture independence in our children. We gradually empower them to take on age-appropriate responsibilities, make decisions and learn from their experiences. By fostering independence, we equip them with essential life skills, such as problem-solving, decision-making and critical thinking. We guide them as they navigate the complexities of life, always ready to offer guidance and support when needed.

SETTING BOUNDARIES

While we strive to be supportive guides, it is also essential to set healthy boundaries. Boundaries provide structure, safety and guidance for our children. They teach them respect for themselves and others, and help them understand the consequences of their actions. By setting clear boundaries with love and consistency, we create a sense of security and promote responsible behavior.

EMBRACING LIFELONG LEARNING

In our role as guides, we foster a love for learning in ourselves and our children. We encourage a mindset of curiosity, exploration and continuous growth. By embracing lifelong learning together, we demonstrate that knowledge extends far beyond formal education. We inspire our children to be curious, ask questions and seek knowledge from a variety of sources. Together, we embark on a journey of discovery and intellectual enrichment.

In the beautiful role of guiding our children, we recognise that our purpose is not to control but to provide a loving, supportive and empowering presence. We navigate this journey with compassion, respect and an unwavering belief in our children's potential. As moms, we understand that our guidance shapes their lives, and we embrace this responsibility with love, nurturing their individuality and empowering them to soar to great heights.

Love becomes the driving force behind our actions, guiding us to make decisions that are rooted in compassion, kindness and understanding.

THE SUPER FUEL OF LOVE

Nurturing heart-centred connections

Love is the essence of motherhood. It is the powerful force that fuels our actions, shapes our relationships and transforms our lives. As mothers, our capacity to love is boundless, and nurturing heart-centred connections with our children and loved ones becomes the cornerstone of a fulfilling and joyful motherhood journey.

THE POWER OF LOVE

Love is more than just an emotion – it is a state of being, a way of relating to ourselves and others. When we approach motherhood from a place of love, we create an environment of warmth, acceptance and support. Love becomes the driving force behind our actions, guiding us to make decisions that are rooted in compassion, kindness and understanding.

UNCONDITIONAL LOVE

Unconditional love is the purest form of love, free from judgement or expectation. It is the type of love that accepts and embraces our children exactly as they are, without trying to mould them into something or expecting them to fulfil our own desires. By practicing unconditional love, we create a safe space for our children to explore, grow and be their authentic selves.

EMOTIONAL CONNECTION

Building emotional connections with our children is vital for their overall wellbeing and development. It involves being fully present with them, listening attentively and validating their feelings and experiences. By creating a nurturing environment where they feel seen, heard and understood, we foster trust and emotional intimacy, laying the foundation for a deep and meaningful relationship.

EMPATHY AND COMPASSION

Empathy and compassion are essential qualities in nurturing heart-centred connections. As mothers, we strive to understand our children's experiences, perspectives and emotions. By putting ourselves in their shoes and seeing the world through their eyes, we cultivate empathy and compassion. These qualities enable us to respond with kindness and support, fostering a sense of belonging and love within our family.

THE LANGUAGE OF LOVE

Love is not only expressed through words but also through our actions and presence. Engaging in acts of love, such as cuddling, playing and spending quality time together, communicates our affection and creates lasting memories. Additionally, expressing verbal affirmations of love, appreciation and encouragement uplifts our children's spirits and strengthens the bond between us.

SELF-LOVE AND SELF-CARE

Nurturing heart-centred connections begins with cultivating love for ourselves. Self-love and self-care are essential practices for replenishing our own energy and wellbeing, enabling us to show up as the best versions of ourselves for our children. By prioritising self-care, setting boundaries and practicing self-compassion, we model healthy relationship dynamics and teach our children the importance of self-love.

FORGIVENESS AND HEALING

In any relationship, forgiveness is a powerful tool for healing and strengthening connections. As mothers, we are not immune to making mistakes or experiencing conflicts with our children. By cultivating a culture of forgiveness, we create a space for growth, understanding and healing. Forgiving ourselves and others allows us to move forward with love and compassion, fostering deeper connections and nurturing emotional resilience.

GRATITUDE AND APPRECIATION

Gratitude is the fuel that ignites love and strengthens connections. Expressing gratitude for the little moments, the challenges and the joy that motherhood brings cultivates a positive and loving atmosphere. By acknowledging and appreciating the efforts and qualities of our children, we uplift their spirits and foster a sense of value and belonging.

Love is the super fuel that powers our motherhood journey. By nurturing heart-centred connections through unconditional love, emotional connection, empathy, compassion, acts of love, self-love, forgiveness and gratitude, we create a harmonious and loving environment for our children to thrive.

Positive energy carries a vibration of love, joy and optimism, and it has a profound impact on our children's emotional and psychological development.

RAISING KIDS IN A LOVING ENVIRONMENT

Cultivating positive energy

Creating a loving environment for our children is one of the most significant gifts we can give them. It sets the foundation for their growth, happiness and overall wellbeing. In this chapter, we explore the importance of cultivating positive energy and creating a nurturing atmosphere that fosters love, joy and harmonious relationships within our families.

THE POWER OF POSITIVE ENERGY

Energy is an invisible force that permeates every aspect of our lives, including our interactions with our children. Positive energy carries a vibration of love, joy and optimism, and it has a profound impact on our children's emotional and psychological development. When we cultivate positive energy within ourselves and our homes, we create an uplifting and supportive environment where our children can thrive.

CULTIVATING SELF-AWARENESS

The first step in cultivating positive energy is developing self-awareness. By becoming attuned to our thoughts, emotions and energy levels, we can identify any negative patterns or blocks that may hinder our ability to create a loving environment. Self-awareness allows us to take responsibility for our own energy and make conscious choices to shift towards positivity and love.

MINDFUL PRESENCE

Being fully present with our children is a powerful way to cultivate positive energy. When we are fully engaged in the present moment, we create a deep connection and a sense of safety for our children. Mindfulness practices such as deep breathing, meditation and conscious parenting help us to anchor ourselves in the present and show up with loving awareness for our children.

CREATING SACRED SPACES

Designating specific spaces within our homes as sacred spaces can significantly impact the energy and atmosphere within them. These spaces can be as simple as a cosy corner with cushions and soft lighting, or a designated area for quiet reflection and meditation. By creating sacred spaces, we invite a sense of peace, tranquility and positive energy into our homes.

POSITIVE COMMUNICATION

Communication plays a vital role in fostering positive energy within our families. It involves not only what we say but also how we say it. Choosing words that uplift, encourage and inspire our children helps to create a loving and supportive atmosphere. Active listening, empathy and open-hearted communication build trust and strengthen the connection between parent and child.

RITUALS AND TRADITIONS

Rituals and traditions hold a special place in creating a loving environment. These meaningful practices bring family members together, foster a sense of belonging and create lasting memories. Whether it's a weekly family game night, a shared mealtime or a bedtime routine filled with loving rituals, these traditions infuse our homes with positive energy and create a sense of togetherness.

NURTURING POSITIVE RELATIONSHIPS

The quality of our relationships with our partners, extended family and friends also impacts the energy within our homes. Nurturing positive relationships involves cultivating love, respect and open communication. By surrounding ourselves and our children with supportive and uplifting individuals, we create a positive social network that reinforces the loving environment we strive to create.

EMBRACING PLAYFULNESS AND JOY

Playfulness and joy are powerful catalysts for positive energy. As mothers, we can infuse our interactions with our children with lightheartedness, laughter and fun. Engaging in playful activities, creating opportunities for spontaneous joy and embracing a sense of humour create an atmosphere that is conducive to love and happiness.

PRACTICING GRATITUDE

Gratitude is a transformative practice that can shift our energy from scarcity to abundance. By cultivating gratitude within ourselves and encouraging our children to express gratitude, we foster a positive outlook on life and invite more blessings into our homes. Gratitude helps us appreciate the present moment and recognise the love and beauty that surround us.

When we love our children unconditionally, we accept and embrace them for who they are, without imposing expectations or conditions.

LEADING WITH LOVE

Nurturing confident leaders

As mothers, our role extends beyond the present moment. We have the extraordinary opportunity to shape our children into confident leaders who will positively impact the world. By leading with love and without fear, we lay the foundation for their future success, happiness and ability to navigate life's challenges. In this chapter, we explore the profound impact of unconditional love and how it shapes our children's journey towards leadership.

THE POWER OF UNCONDITIONAL LOVE

Unconditional love is a powerful force that has the potential to transform lives. When we love our children unconditionally, we accept and embrace them for who they are, without imposing expectations or conditions. Unconditional love creates a safe and nurturing environment where our children can explore, learn and grow without the fear of judgement or rejection. This foundation of love empowers them to develop a strong sense of self-worth and confidence.

INSTILLING CONFIDENCE

Confidence is a key attribute of successful leaders. By fostering a loving and supportive environment, we instil confidence in our children from an early age. When they feel unconditionally loved and accepted, they develop a belief in themselves and their abilities. We encourage their exploration, celebrate their achievements and provide guidance and encouragement when faced with challenges. Through our unwavering support, we nurture their confidence and belief in their own potential.

MODELING FEARLESSNESS

As mothers, we play a crucial role in modelling fearlessness for our children. When we lead with love and without fear, we demonstrate courage and resilience in the face of adversity. We show them that it is okay to make mistakes, that failures are opportunities for growth and that they have the strength to overcome obstacles. By embracing our own vulnerability and facing challenges head-on, we teach our children the importance of courage and inspire them to navigate life with confidence.

ENCOURAGING SELF-EXPRESSION

Confident leaders are unafraid to express themselves authentically. By creating an environment where self-expression is encouraged and celebrated, we empower our children to find their unique voice and share their thoughts, ideas and creativity with the world. We listen attentively to their words, validate their feelings and support their interests and passions. By nurturing their self-expression, we lay the groundwork for their leadership journey.

FOSTERING INDEPENDENCE AND DECISION-MAKING

Leadership is often synonymous with making decisions and taking responsibility for one's actions. As mothers, we can foster independence and decision-making skills in our children by providing them with age-appropriate opportunities to make choices and solve problems. By allowing them to experience the consequences of their decisions in a safe environment, we equip them with the tools and confidence to navigate decision-making with wisdom and clarity.

PROMOTING EMPATHY AND COMPASSION

Effective leaders understand the importance of empathy and compassion. By teaching our children the value of empathy, we cultivate their ability to understand and connect with others' emotions and experiences. We encourage acts of kindness, teach them to listen with an open heart and foster a sense of social responsibility. Through these practices, we raise compassionate leaders who lead with love and consider the wellxz-being of others.

BUILDING RESILIENCE

Resilience is a vital quality for leaders, as it enables them to bounce back from setbacks and face challenges with determination. By creating a loving and supportive environment, we help our children develop resilience by providing them with a secure base from which to explore the world. We offer them guidance, teach them problem-solving skills and validate their emotions. Through these experiences, they learn to adapt, persevere and grow stronger in the face of adversity.

HEALING FROM THE PAST

As mothers, we have the opportunity to break the cycle of fear and limitations that may have been present in our own upbringing by choosing to lead with unconditional love.

Each child is born with their own path to navigate and lessons to learn. As guardians, it is crucial to recognise and respect their individual journeys.

GUARDIANS OF LOVE

Creating a sacred space for our children

As mothers, we are entrusted with the sacred task of being the guardians of our children's wellbeing and growth. It is essential to remind ourselves regularly that our children are on their unique journey, encountering their own life lessons and experiences. Our role is to love them unconditionally and provide a safe, nurturing space for them to come home to. In this chapter, we explore the significance of being guardians of love and creating a sacred space for our children.

RECOGNISING THEIR INDIVIDUAL JOURNEYS

Each child is born with their own path to navigate and lessons to learn. As guardians, it is crucial to recognise and respect their individual journeys. We must resist the urge to control or impose our own expectations upon them. Instead, we offer guidance, support and unconditional love as they discover their unique purpose and passions. By acknowledging their autonomy, we empower them to develop their sense of identity and take ownership of their lives.

UNCONDITIONAL LOVE AS A FOUNDATION

Unconditional love is the bedrock upon which we build a sacred space for our children. It is a love that accepts and embraces them for who they are, regardless of their choices or circumstances. Through unconditional love, we create an unwavering support system that fosters their emotional wellbeing, self-esteem and resilience. It is within this space that they can freely explore, express themselves and grow into the individuals they are destined to become.

BEING A SAFE HAVEN

In a world filled with uncertainties and challenges, our role as guardians is to be a safe haven for our children. We cultivate an environment where they feel secure, loved and understood. We provide them with a sanctuary where they can retreat, express their emotions and seek solace. By being present and attuned to their needs, we offer them the comfort and reassurance they need to navigate the ups and downs of life.

ACTIVE LISTENING AND EMPATHY

Creating a sacred space involves active listening and empathy. We take the time to truly hear and understand our children, both their words and their unspoken emotions. Through active listening, we validate their experiences, concerns and joys. We show empathy by putting ourselves in their shoes, acknowledging their feelings and offering our unwavering support. This compassionate presence allows them to open up, trust and feel seen and heard.

NURTURING EMOTIONAL WELLBEING

Emotional wellbeing is a vital aspect of creating a sacred space for our children. We teach them emotional intelligence by modelling healthy emotional expression and providing tools for emotional regulation. We encourage them to identify and express their feelings, validating their emotions without judgement. By nurturing their emotional wellbeing, we equip them with the tools to navigate their inner world and form healthy relationships.

CULTIVATING OPEN COMMUNICATION

Open communication is the lifeblood of a sacred space. We create an atmosphere where our children feel comfortable expressing their thoughts, concerns and dreams openly. We encourage dialogue, ask open-ended questions and genuinely listen to their responses. By fostering open communication, we foster trust and strengthen the bond between us and our children. It becomes a safe space where they can freely share their ideas, seek guidance and receive loving support.

ENCOURAGING PERSONAL GROWTH

We support and encourage our children's personal growth and self-discovery. We provide opportunities for them to explore their interests, talents and passions. We expose them to new experiences, encourage them to take healthy risks, and celebrate their achievements. By nurturing their personal growth, we empower them to develop their unique strengths, talents and values.

TEACHING RESILIENCE AND INDEPENDENCE

Creating a sacred space includes teaching our children resilience and independence. We encourage them to face challenges, learn from failures and develop problem-solving skills. We empower them to make decisions, take responsibility for their actions and learn from the consequences. By fostering resilience and independence, we equip them with the tools to navigate life's obstacles with confidence and adaptability.

As guardians of love, we have the privilege and responsibility of creating a sacred space for our children. Through unconditional love, being a safe haven, active listening, empathy, nurturing emotional wellbeing, open communication, encouraging personal growth and teaching resilience and independence, we provide them with the foundation they need to flourish on their individual journeys. Let us embrace this role with gratitude and dedication, knowing that we are shaping the future leaders of tomorrow.

Tough love is not about being harsh or punitive; it is about setting boundaries and guiding our children back onto their path when they have strayed too far.

BALANCING LOVE AND BOUNDARIES

Nurturing with tough love

As mothers, our love for our children knows no bounds. We want nothing more than to see them happy, fulfilled and on the right path. However, there are moments when tough love becomes necessary. Tough love is not about being harsh or punitive; it is about setting boundaries and guiding our children back onto their path when they have strayed too far. In this chapter, we explore the delicate balance between love and tough love, and the role of intuition in knowing when to apply each.

THE POWER OF LOVE

Love is the foundation of our relationship with our children. It is the force that connects us deeply and unconditionally. Our love provides a safe haven for them to explore, learn and grow. It is the wellspring of support, encouragement and understanding. Love offers a nurturing space for our children to develop their unique potential and flourish.

SETTING BOUNDARIES

While love is essential, setting boundaries is equally important. Boundaries create structure, safety and guidance for our children. They help define expectations, responsibilities and consequences. Boundaries teach our children about personal limits, self-discipline and respect for others. By setting boundaries, we empower our children to make healthy choices, develop resilience and understand the importance of accountability.

THE ART OF TOUGH LOVE

Tough love is an art that requires careful consideration and intuition. It is not about being harsh or withholding affection; it is about showing our children the way back onto their path when they have veered off course. Tough love involves implementing consequences, enforcing rules and providing guidance with firmness and clarity. It is an act of love that helps our children learn from their mistakes, take responsibility for their actions, and grow into responsible individuals.

TRUSTING INTUITION

Intuition plays a vital role in navigating the balance between love and tough love. As mothers, we possess a deep knowing about our children. We can sense when they have gone too far, when they need guidance and when they need a gentle push to reclaim their true potential. Trusting our intuition allows us to discern the right moments to employ tough love while maintaining a foundation of love and support.

FINDING THE RIGHT APPROACH

Applying tough love requires finding the right approach that resonates with each individual child. Every child is unique, and what works for one may not work for another. It is important to consider their temperament, communication style and emotional needs. Some children may respond best to direct conversations and clear expectations, while others may benefit from creative problem-solving or reflective exercises. Finding the right approach ensures that tough love is effective in guiding our children back onto their path.

COMMUNICATION AND UNDERSTANDING

Effective communication is key when practicing tough love. It is crucial to explain the reasons behind the boundaries, consequences and expectations. Open and honest dialogue allows our children to understand our intentions, learn from their mistakes and make positive changes. By fostering a climate of understanding and respect, we create a safe space for our children to share their thoughts, concerns and perspectives.

MAINTAINING CONNECTION

Even in moments of tough love, it is essential to maintain a deep connection with our children. We communicate our unwavering love and support, assuring them that our actions stem from a place of caring and guiding. We provide comfort, reassurance and encouragement during challenging times. By maintaining connection, we build trust and create a solid foundation for our children to lean on as they navigate their own paths.

BALANCING SELF-CARE

Practicing tough love can be emotionally challenging for mothers. It is crucial to balance self-care alongside our commitment to guiding our children. Taking care of our own emotional wellbeing, seeking support when needed and prioritising self-care activities rejuvenate our energy and allow us to be the best version of ourselves.

Love is not just a mere emotion; it is a powerful energy that can be consciously directed towards our children.

HEALING WITH LOVE

Nurturing our children with compassionate energy

As mothers, we possess an incredible power to heal and nurture our children with the energy of love. Love is a transformative force that has the ability to mend wounds, soothe pain and foster growth and resilience. In this chapter, we explore the profound impact of pouring loving energy into our children's lives, and how it can create a healing and nurturing environment for their physical, emotional and spiritual wellbeing.

THE POWER OF LOVING ENERGY

Love is not just a mere emotion; it is a powerful energy that can be consciously directed towards our children. When we infuse our interactions, words and actions with love, we create an environment that supports their healing and growth. Love has the ability to create a sense of safety, trust and connection, allowing our children to flourish and thrive in all aspects of their lives.

UNCONDITIONAL LOVE

Unconditional love is a pure and unwavering form of love that accepts and embraces our children exactly as they are, without judgement or conditions. When we offer our children unconditional love, we create a space where they feel seen, heard and valued. This love becomes a source of strength and resilience, empowering them to navigate challenges, build healthy relationships and embrace their true selves.

HEALING EMOTIONAL WOUNDS

Our children may encounter emotional wounds along their journey, such as heartbreak, disappointment or fear. By pouring loving energy into their lives, we provide a healing balm for these wounds. Love helps to create a sense of emotional safety and support, allowing them to express their feelings without judgement or shame. Through our love, we validate their emotions, offer comfort and guide them towards emotional healing and growth.

NURTURING PHYSICAL WELLBEING

Love has a profound impact on our children's physical wellbeing. When we prioritise their health and wellness with a foundation of love, we create a nurturing environment for their bodies to thrive. This includes providing nutritious meals, encouraging physical activity and attending to their health care needs with compassion. By infusing our actions with love, we foster a sense of self-care and wellbeing that will serve them throughout their lives.

CREATING RITUALS OF LOVE

Rituals and traditions infused with love create lasting memories and strengthen the bond between parent and child. These can be simple acts, such as bedtime rituals, family meals or shared activities that are filled with love, presence and connection. These rituals become touchstones in our children's lives, reminding them of the love and support they have from their mothers. By creating these rituals, we cultivate a sense of security and belonging, promoting their emotional and psychological wellbeing.

TRANSMITTING POSITIVE ENERGY

Our energy as mothers has a profound impact on our children. When we consciously transmit positive and loving energy, we uplift their spirits and create an atmosphere of joy and positivity. Our words, gestures and presence can serve as a source of inspiration, motivation and encouragement. By radiating love and positive energy, we empower our children to believe in themselves, overcome challenges and embrace their own innate potential.

Pouring loving energy into our children's lives is a profound gift that has the power to heal, nurture and transform. By offering them unconditional love, healing emotional wounds, nurturing their physical wellbeing, creating rituals of love and transmitting positive energy, we become catalysts for their growth, wellbeing and happiness. Let us embrace the power of love and pour it abundantly into the lives of our precious children, creating a world filled with healing, joy and limitless possibilities.

By embracing love as a transformative force, you can create a nurturing and supportive environment where your children can flourish.

LOVE AS A TRANSFORMATIVE FORCE

Nurturing deep connections with your children

Love is the most powerful and transformative force in the world, and as a mother, you have the incredible opportunity to cultivate deep and meaningful connections with your children through love. In this chapter, we explore the profound impact of love in your role as a mother and how nurturing these connections can shape the lives of your children. By embracing love as a transformative force, you can create a nurturing and supportive environment where your children can flourish.

UNCONDITIONAL LOVE

Embracing acceptance: Unconditional love means accepting your children for who they are, without judgement or conditions. Celebrate their uniqueness and let them know that they are loved just as they are.

Emotional support: Show empathy and understanding when your children face challenges or difficult emotions. Be a safe space for them to express themselves and provide comfort and reassurance.

OPEN COMMUNICATION

Active listening: Practice active listening by giving your full attention when your children are speaking. Create a non-judgemental and open space for them to share their thoughts, feelings and experiences.

Empathy and validation: Validate your children's emotions and experiences, letting them know that their feelings are heard and understood. Empathise with them and provide guidance and support when needed.

QUALITY TIME

Dedicated attention: Set aside dedicated time to be fully present with your children. Engage in activities that they enjoy and create cherished memories together.

One-on-one connection: Foster individual connections with each of your children by spending one-on-one time with them. This allows for deeper bonding and a sense of being seen and valued.

ACTS OF KINDNESS

Small gestures: Show love through daily acts of kindness, such as hugs, kisses, compliments or surprise notes. These small gestures go a long way in nurturing your connection with your children.

Random acts of kindness: Encourage your children to engage in random acts of kindness as well, cultivating a culture of compassion and empathy within your family.

SETTING BOUNDARIES WITH LOVE

Teaching values: Set clear boundaries that align with your family values and explain the reasoning behind them. Help your children understand the importance of boundaries as a way to show love and respect for themselves and others.

Discipline with love: When discipline is necessary, approach it with love and compassion. Use it as an opportunity to teach valuable lessons and guide your children towards making positive choices.

LEADING BY EXAMPLE

Model love and kindness: Be a role model by demonstrating love, kindness and respect in your actions and interactions with others. Your children learn from observing your behaviour and will emulate the love they see in you.

Self-love and self-care: Show your children the importance of self-love and self-care. Take care of yourself physically, mentally and emotionally, demonstrating that love starts from within.

Love is the foundation of your relationship with your children and has the power to transform their lives. By embracing unconditional love, fostering open communication, dedicating quality time, practicing acts of kindness, setting boundaries with love and leading by example, you create a nurturing and supportive environment where your children can thrive. Embrace love as a transformative force and watch as deep connections and lasting bonds are formed, enriching the lives of both you and your children.

By understanding that resistance is a normal part of their journey, we can approach these situations with empathy, patience and love.

LOVING THROUGH RESISTANCE

Nurturing relationships in challenging times

Motherhood is not always smooth sailing. It comes with its fair share of challenges, including tantrums, teenage rebellion, life lessons, financial struggles and other problems. However, it is during these times of resistance that our love is needed the most. In this chapter, we explore how to navigate and love our children through these challenging moments.

UNDERSTANDING THE NATURE OF RESISTANCE

Resistance is a natural part of growth and development. It manifests differently at various stages of our children's lives, from the terrible twos to the teenage years and beyond. Tantrums, rebellion and pushing boundaries are ways for children to assert their independence and test their limits. By understanding that resistance is a normal part of their journey, we can approach these situations with empathy, patience and love.

CULTIVATING EMPATHY AND COMPASSION

Empathy and compassion are powerful tools in navigating resistance. Put yourself in your child's shoes and try to understand their perspective. Validate their emotions and let them know that you are there for them, even when their behaviour is challenging. By showing empathy, we create a safe space for our children to express themselves and find healthy ways to cope.

EFFECTIVE COMMUNICATION AND ACTIVE LISTENING

Communication is key in any relationship, especially during times of resistance. Engage in open, honest and respectful conversations with your children. Practice active listening, giving them your full attention and validating their feelings. Create a safe and non-judgemental environment where they can express themselves freely. By fostering effective communication, we build trust and strengthen the bond with our children.

TEACHING LIFE LESSONS

Resistance often presents opportunities for valuable life lessons. Rather than seeing challenges as obstacles, view them as chances for growth and learning. Guide your children through difficult situations, offering guidance and support. Teach them the importance of taking responsibility for their actions. By helping them navigate these challenges, you equip them with essential life skills that will serve them well into adulthood.

NAVIGATING FINANCIAL STRUGGLES

Financial struggles can create stress and tension within a family. It is important to approach these challenges with honesty and transparency. Involve your children in age-appropriate discussions about money, helping them understand the value of financial responsibility. Find creative ways to teach them about budgeting, saving and making informed decisions. By fostering financial literacy, you empower them to develop healthy attitudes towards money and navigate future financial challenges.

MAINTAINING BOUNDARIES AND CONSISTENCY

During times of resistance, it is crucial to maintain boundaries and consistency. Children thrive in environments with clear expectations and consistent discipline. Set firm but fair boundaries, and enforce them consistently. This provides a sense of security and stability for your children, helping them understand the consequences of their actions and learn self-discipline.

MODELLING HEALTHY COPING MECHANISMS

As mothers, we are powerful role models for our children. During challenging times, it is essential to model healthy coping mechanisms. Show them how to manage stress, frustration and disappointment in constructive ways. Practice self-care, engage in activities that bring you joy and seek support when needed. By demonstrating healthy coping strategies, you teach your children the importance of self-care and resilience.

CELEBRATING THE VICTORIES

Amidst the challenges, it is crucial to celebrate the victories, no matter how small. Acknowledge and appreciate your children's efforts and achievements. Highlight their strengths and successes, reinforcing positive behaviour and growth. Celebrating the victories builds their self-esteem and motivates them to continue on their journey of growth and self-discovery.

In conclusion, loving our children through resistance requires empathy, effective communication, teaching life lessons, navigating financial struggles, maintaining boundaries and consistency, modelling healthy coping mechanisms and celebrating their victories. By approaching these challenging moments with love, understanding and patience, we nurture strong and resilient relationships with our children, helping them navigate life's ups and downs with confidence and love.

By cultivating a culture of kindness, we create an environment where love and compassion thrive.

LOVE IN ACTION

Radiating compassion and kindness as a mom

Love is the essence of motherhood, and it is through the active practice of compassion and kindness that we embody the transformative power of love in our role as moms. Love in action goes beyond mere words or feelings; it is about expressing love through our thoughts, words and deeds, creating a nurturing and harmonious environment for our children to thrive. In this chapter, we explore the profound impact of radiating compassion and kindness as a mom and how it shapes the lives of our children.

THE POWER OF COMPASSION

Compassion is the ability to understand and empathise with the emotions and experiences of others, including our children. When we approach motherhood with compassion, we cultivate a deep sense of connection, understanding and acceptance. Compassion allows us to see beyond our children's behaviours and challenges, recognising their inherent worth and supporting them through love and kindness.

PRACTICING SELF-COMPASSION

Before we can extend compassion to others, including our children, we must first practice self-compassion. Self-compassion involves treating ourselves with kindness, understanding and forgiveness. By nurturing our own wellbeing and self-acceptance, we create a reservoir of love that overflows onto our children. Taking care of ourselves allows us to show up as the best versions of ourselves, modelling self-love and compassion to our children.

EMPATHY: STEPPING INTO THEIR SHOES

Empathy is the ability to understand and share the feelings of others. As moms, cultivating empathy allows us to step into our children's shoes, seeing the world from their perspective. By listening attentively, validating their emotions and offering support, we create a safe space for our children to express themselves authentically. Through empathy, we foster deep connections and nurture emotional wellbeing.

KINDNESS IN ACTION

Kindness is a powerful force that can transform relationships and create a positive impact in our children's lives. Simple acts of kindness, such as a loving touch, a warm smile or a gentle word, have the power to uplift and nurture our children's spirits. Kindness in action also involves modelling respectful communication, resolving conflicts peacefully and extending kindness to ourselves and others. By cultivating a culture of kindness, we create an environment where love and compassion thrive.

TEACHING EMOTIONAL INTELLIGENCE

Emotional intelligence is a vital skill that equips our children with the tools to understand, manage and express their emotions in healthy ways. As moms, we play a crucial role in teaching emotional intelligence by fostering open communication, validating emotions and providing guidance on emotional regulation. Through these practices, we empower our children to navigate their emotions with compassion and empathy towards themselves and others.

THE RIPPLE EFFECT OF LOVE

Love in action has a ripple effect that extends beyond our immediate family. As our children witness and experience the love and kindness we embody, they carry those qualities into their interactions with others, spreading love and compassion throughout their lives. By nurturing a loving and kind environment at home, we contribute to a more compassionate and harmonious society.

GRATITUDE AND APPRECIATION

Expressing gratitude and appreciation for our children and their unique qualities nurtures a deep sense of love and connection. By regularly acknowledging and celebrating their accomplishments, efforts and growth, we reinforce their sense of self-worth and cultivate a positive and loving atmosphere. Gratitude also serves as a reminder of the blessings and joys that motherhood brings, fostering a grateful heart.

Radiating compassion and kindness as a mom is a transformative practice that shapes the lives of our children and creates a ripple effect of love in the world. By practicing self-compassion, cultivating empathy, showing kindness in action, teaching emotional intelligence and fostering gratitude and appreciation, we create a nurturing and loving environment for our children to flourish. Let us embrace the power of love in action, infusing our motherhood journey with compassion and kindness that transcends boundaries and enriches the lives of those around us.

Practicing active listening: Show your children the importance of truly listening to others.

EMBODYING LOVE

Modelling empathy and kindness for your children

As moms, we have a profound influence on our children's develop-ment, not only through our words but also through our actions. One of the most powerful ways we can shape their character and nurture their hearts is by embodying love in our daily lives. In this chapter, we explore the transformative power of modelling empathy and kindness and how it impacts our children's growth and the world around them.

THE RIPPLE EFFECT OF LOVE

Understanding the impact: Recognise that your words, gestures and behaviours have a lasting impact on your children. Every act of love and kindness ripples outward, shaping their perception of the world and influencing how they treat others.

CULTIVATING EMPATHY

Practicing active listening: Show your children the importance of truly listening to others. Practice active listening by giving your full attention, showing empathy and validating their feelings and experiences.

Encouraging perspective-taking: Help your children develop empathy by encouraging them to see things from others' perspectives. Teach them to consider how their actions may impact others and to respond with kindness and understanding.

MODELLING KINDNESS

Random acts of kindness: Engage in random acts of kindness as a family, such as helping a neighbour, volunteering together or leaving uplifting notes for others. Demonstrate that even small acts of kindness can make a big difference.

Modelling inclusive behaviour: Teach your children the value of inclusivity and acceptance by modelling inclusive behaviour in your interactions with others. Show them the beauty of diversity and the importance of treating everyone with kindness and respect.

PRACTICING SELF-COMPASSION

Being gentle with yourself: Show your children the importance of self-love and self-compassion by being gentle with yourself. Embrace self-care practices, speak kindly to yourself and demonstrate the value of setting healthy boundaries.

Apologising and making amends: When you make a mistake or act unkindly, model accountability and emotional responsibility by apologising to your children and making amends. Teach them that mistakes are opportunities for growth and learning.

TEACHING CONFLICT RESOLUTION

Peaceful communication: Teach your children healthy communication skills, such as active listening, expressing emotions and resolving conflicts peacefully. Model effective communication strategies in your own interactions to create a harmonious environment at home.

Mediating conflicts: Act as a mediator when conflicts arise between siblings or other family members. Teach your children strategies for finding common ground, understanding different perspectives and working toward peaceful resolutions.

NURTURING EMPATHY AND KINDNESS IN EVERYDAY LIFE

Storytelling and literature: Use storytelling and literature to nurture empathy and kindness in your children. Choose books that promote compassion, empathy and understanding, and engage in meaningful discussions about the characters' experiences.

Gratitude and acts of service: Cultivate a spirit of gratitude and service by engaging your children in acts of kindness toward others. Encourage them to express gratitude, lend a helping hand or participate in community service projects.

By embodying love, empathy and kindness in our daily lives, we create a nurturing environment for our children to grow and thrive. Through our actions and modelling, we teach them the value of compassion, empathy and inclusive behaviour. By nurturing their hearts and guiding them to be loving and kind individuals, we contribute to a more compassionate and harmonious world. Embrace the power of embodying love and let it shine through your words, actions and interactions with your children and others.

Inspire your children to explore the world around them with a sense of wonder and curiosity.

EMBRACING THE LOVE OF LIFE

Cultivating a harmonious relationship

As mothers, we have the incredible opportunity to not only love our children but also teach them how to love life itself. When we show our children the beauty and wonder that life holds, we open the door for them to experience joy, gratitude and a deep connection to the world around them. In this chapter, we explore the importance of nurturing a love for life in our children and how it can bring abundance, fulfilment and a sense of purpose to their lives.

FINDING JOY IN THE PRESENT MOMENT

Embracing mindfulness: Teach your children the power of being fully present in each moment. Encourage them to engage their senses, notice the beauty around them and savour the simple pleasures that life offers.

Cultivating gratitude: Foster a sense of gratitude in your children by encouraging them to appreciate the small things in life. Help them create gratitude practices such as keeping a gratitude journal or sharing daily gratitudes around the dinner table.

INSTILLING A SENSE OF WONDER AND CURIOSITY

Encouraging exploration: Inspire your children to explore the world around them with a sense of wonder and curiosity. Take them on nature walks, visit museums or engage in activities that spark their imagination and desire to learn.

Nurturing creativity: Support your children's creative pursuits and allow them to express themselves freely. Encourage them to engage in activities such as drawing, writing or playing music, which can ignite their passion for life.

TEACHING RESILIENCE AND GRATITUDE

Embracing challenges as opportunities: Teach your children that challenges and setbacks are part of life's journey. Help them develop resilience and a positive mindset by reframing difficulties as opportunities for growth and learning.

Practicing gratitude in difficult times: Encourage your children to find gratitude even in challenging situations. Teach them to focus on the lessons learned and the strength they gain from overcoming obstacles.

CULTIVATING A CONNECTION WITH NATURE

Spending time outdoors: Foster a love for nature by spending time outdoors with your children. Take them on hikes, have picnics in the park or simply play in the backyard. Help them develop a deep appreciation for the natural world and its wonders.

Teaching environmental responsibility: Instil in your children a sense of responsibility towards the environment. Teach them about conservation, recycling and the importance of taking care of our planet.

NURTURING POSITIVE RELATIONSHIPS

Modelling love and kindness: Show your children the importance of loving and kind relationships by modelling healthy connections in your own life. Demonstrate empathy, compassion and respect in your interactions with others.

Encouraging meaningful connections: Teach your children the value of meaningful relationships by encouraging them to cultivate friendships based on mutual respect, support and shared values.

EMBRACING LIFE'S ADVENTURES

Trying new experiences: Encourage your children to step outside their comfort zones and try new things. Whether it's learning a new hobby, joining a club or embarking on an adventure, help them embrace the excitement and growth that comes from new experiences.

Embracing spontaneity: Allow room for spontaneity and playfulness in your daily lives. Let go of rigid schedules occasionally and embrace moments of joy, laughter and unplanned adventures.

By nurturing a love for life in our children, we gift them with the ability to find joy, purpose and fulfilment in all that they do. As mothers, we have the privilege of showing our children how to embrace each moment, find gratitude in the simplest pleasures and forge meaningful connections. By instilling a love for life, we equip our children with the tools to navigate challenges, appreciate the beauty around them and live a life filled with love, abundance and limitless possibilities.

Gratitude

When we cultivate an attitude of gratitude, we shift our focus from what is lacking to what is abundant and present in our lives.

GRATITUDE AS A LIFE HACK

Reconnecting with the flow of manifesting

Gratitude is a powerful tool that can transform our lives in remarkable ways. It is not just a fleeting feeling of appreciation; it is a way of being, a state of mind that opens the floodgates of abundance and allows us to reconnect with the flow of manifesting. In this chapter, we delve into the profound impact of gratitude and explore how it can become a life hack for moms, helping us tap into the limitless possibilities that await us.

THE POWER OF GRATITUDE

Gratitude is like a magnet that draws more blessings into our lives. When we cultivate an attitude of gratitude, we shift our focus from what is lacking to what is abundant and present in our lives. It is a practice of recognising and appreciating the blessings, big and small, that surround us. By acknowledging and expressing gratitude, we create a positive energy that attracts more positive experiences.

RECONNECTING WITH THE PRESENT MOMENT

In the whirlwind of motherhood, it is easy to get caught up in the chaos and lose sight of the present moment. Gratitude serves as an anchor, pulling us back into the here and now. When we practice gratitude, we become fully present, savouring the beauty and joy that exists in each moment. It helps us slow down, take a deep breath and appreciate the precious moments we share with our children.

SHIFTING PERSPECTIVES

Gratitude has the power to transform our perspectives. It allows us to see challenges as opportunities for growth and lessons in disguise. Instead of dwelling on what went wrong, we can focus on the lessons learned and the resilience we develop in the process. By shifting our perspectives through gratitude, we cultivate a positive mindset that enables us to navigate the ups and downs of motherhood with grace and resilience.

AMPLIFYING ABUNDANCE

Gratitude is the gateway to abundance. When we express gratitude for what we already have, we send a powerful message to the universe that we are ready to receive more. It is a shift from scarcity thinking to an abundance mindset. By recognising the abundance in our lives, whether it is love, health, support or opportunities, we open ourselves up to receive even more blessings.

THE RIPPLE EFFECT OF GRATITUDE

Practicing gratitude not only benefits us but also has a ripple effect on those around us, especially our children. When our children see us embodying gratitude, they learn the art of appreciation and the power of positive thinking. It becomes a part of their worldview, shaping their attitudes and actions. By modelling gratitude, we create a positive and nurturing environment that fosters their own sense of appreciation and abundance.

CULTIVATING A GRATITUDE PRACTICE

Incorporating gratitude into our daily lives requires practice and intention. It can take many forms, such as keeping a gratitude journal, expressing gratitude through prayers or affirmations or simply pausing to reflect on the things we are grateful for each day. Experiment with different approaches and find what resonates with you. The key is consistency and genuine appreciation.

EMBRACING THE FLOW OF MANIFESTING

Gratitude is a powerful tool for manifesting our desires. As we express gratitude for what we have, we align ourselves with the energy of abundance and attract more of what we desire into our lives. It is not about striving and chasing after what we lack; it is about embracing the flow and trusting that everything we need is already within our reach.

Gratitude is a life hack that allows us to reconnect with the flow of manifesting. By practicing gratitude, we shift our perspectives, amplify abundance, cultivate a positive environment for ourselves and our children and open ourselves up to receive more blessings. Let us embrace the power of gratitude and allow it to become an integral part of our daily lives, bringing us closer to the life of joy, fulfilment and abundance we deserve.

The gratitude ripple effect is a transformative force that can bring joy, appreciation and resilience into your motherhood journey.

THE GRATITUDE RIPPLE EFFECT

Spreading joy and appreciation in your motherhood journey

Gratitude is a powerful practice that has the ability to transform our perspective and enhance our wellbeing. As a mother, cultivating a mindset of gratitude can have a profound impact on your experience and the lives of your children. In this chapter, we explore the gratitude ripple effect and how spreading joy and appreciation can enrich your motherhood journey. By embracing gratitude, you can create a positive and uplifting environment that fosters happiness, resilience and deep connections with your children.

THE POWER OF GRATITUDE

Shifting perspective: Gratitude allows you to shift your focus from what's lacking to what's present in your life. It helps you recognise and appreciate the blessings and joys, no matter how small they may seem.

Cultivating positivity: When you practice gratitude, you invite more positivity into your life. It uplifts your mood, reduces stress and creates a harmonious atmosphere within your family.

GRATITUDE PRACTICES FOR MOMS

Gratitude journalling: Set aside a few moments each day to write down things you are grateful for. It could be as simple as a smile from your child, a supportive partner or a beautiful sunrise. Reflecting on these moments reinforces the positive aspects of your motherhood journey.

Daily gratitude rituals: Incorporate gratitude into your daily routine. For example, during mealtime or bedtime, encourage each family member to share something they are grateful for that day. This creates a habit of appreciation and fosters a sense of gratitude within your family.

Gratitude walks: Take mindful walks with your children in nature, encouraging them to express gratitude for the beauty around them. Point out the wonders of nature and guide them to appreciate the simple joys that surround them.

TEACHING GRATITUDE TO YOUR CHILDREN

Lead by example: Model gratitude in your own life. Let your children see you expressing appreciation and gratitude for the people, experiences and things that bring you joy. Your actions and attitude serve as powerful lessons for them.

Gratitude conversations: Engage your children in conversations about gratitude. Ask them what they are thankful for and encourage them to express appreciation for the people and things that enrich their lives. This helps them develop a positive and appreciative mindset.

Acts of kindness: Encourage your children to perform acts of kindness as a way of expressing gratitude. This could be writing thank-you notes, doing something thoughtful for a family member or friend or participating in community service projects.

THE GRATITUDE RIPPLE EFFECT

Spreading joy: When you cultivate gratitude within yourself and your family, you create a ripple effect of joy. Your positive energy and appreciation spread to those around you, uplifting their spirits and fostering a sense of connection and wellbeing.

Building resilience: Gratitude helps build resilience in the face of challenges. It teaches your children to focus on the positive aspects of life, even during difficult times, and helps them develop a mindset of resilience and gratitude.

Strengthening relationships: Expressing gratitude fosters deeper connections within your family. When you acknowledge and appreciate the efforts and qualities of your children, you strengthen your bond and create a supportive and loving atmosphere.

The gratitude ripple effect is a transformative force that can bring joy, appreciation and resilience into your motherhood journey. By practicing gratitude, teaching it to your children and spreading the joy of appreciation, you create a positive and uplifting environment where love, happiness and deep connections flourish. Embrace gratitude as a way of life, and watch as the ripple effect of gratitude spreads throughout your family and beyond, enriching the lives of all who are touched by it.

Take time to express genuine appreciation for your children. Let them know how grateful you are for their unique qualities, their love and the joy they bring to your life.

GRATITUDE PRACTICES FOR BUSY MOMS

Cultivating joy and abundance

In the whirlwind of motherhood, it's easy to get caught up in the busyness and challenges of daily life. However, cultivating gratitude is a powerful practice that can bring immense joy, abundance and perspective to our lives as moms. In this chapter, we explore various gratitude practices specifically designed for busy moms, helping us to reconnect with the blessings and find moments of appreciation amidst the chaos.

GRATITUDE JOURNALLING

Begin a gratitude journal: Set aside a few minutes each day to write down three things you are grateful for. It could be something as simple as a smile from your child or a moment of peace in the midst of chaos.

Reflect on your day: Before bed, take a moment to reflect on the day and write down three things that brought you joy or made you feel grateful. This practice helps shift your focus towards the positive aspects of motherhood.

GRATITUDE AFFIRMATIONS

Start your day with gratitude affirmations: Repeat affirmations such as, 'I am grateful for the love and joy my children bring into my life,' or, 'I am grateful for the strength and patience I possess as a mother.' These affirmations set a positive tone for the day ahead.

Express gratitude for challenges: When faced with difficulties, affirm, 'I am grateful for the growth and lessons that come from these challenges. They make me a stronger and wiser mother.'

GRATITUDE RITUALS

Gratitude jar: Keep a jar and slips of paper nearby. Throughout the day, write down moments, experiences or things you feel grateful for and place them in the jar. Whenever you need a boost, read the slips of gratitude and bask in the positive energy.

Gratitude meditation: Set aside a few minutes each day for a gratitude meditation. Focus on your breath and bring to mind things you are grateful for, savouring the emotions and sensations that arise.

FINDING GRATITUDE IN EVERYDAY MOMENTS

Mindful gratitude: Practice being fully present in everyday moments with your children. Take notice of their laughter, the warmth of their hugs or the sound of their voices. Cultivate gratitude for these precious moments that make motherhood so meaningful.

Gratitude for self-care: Acknowledge and appreciate the small acts of self-care you engage in as a busy mom. Whether it's a relaxing bath, a quiet cup of tea or a few moments of solitude, express gratitude for the self-nurturing choices you make.

GRATITUDE IN RELATIONSHIPS

Express gratitude to your children: Take time to express genuine appreciation for your children. Let them know how grateful you are for their unique qualities, their love and the joy they bring to your life.

Appreciate support: Express gratitude to the people who support you in your motherhood journey, whether it's your partner, family members or friends. Acknowledge and thank them for their love, assistance and understanding.

Gratitude practices are essential for busy moms to cultivate joy, abundance and a sense of perspective in their lives. By incorporating gratitude journalling, affirmations, rituals, finding gratitude in everyday moments and expressing gratitude in relationships, we create a positive shift in our mindset and experience the richness of motherhood. Let us embrace the power of gratitude to bring more joy and appreciation into our lives as busy moms.

Encourage your children to express gratitude for the abundance in their lives, whether it's material possessions, experiences, relationships or personal growth

LIVING IN ABUNDANCE

Attracting prosperity and abundance through gratitude

In our journey as moms, we not only want to provide for our children's needs but also teach them about the abundance and prosperity that life has to offer. It's important to cultivate a mindset of abundance and gratitude, both for ourselves and our children, so they can grow up understanding that abundance extends beyond material possessions. In this chapter, we explore how practicing gratitude can help us attract prosperity and abundance into our lives, while also teaching our children about financial responsibility and the true meaning of abundance.

SHIFTING TO AN ABUNDANCE MINDSET

Recognising abundance: Shift your mindset from scarcity to abundance by acknowledging the blessings and abundance already present in your life. Focus on gratitude for the simple joys, experiences and connections that bring richness to your life.

TEACHING FINANCIAL RESPONSIBILITY

Age-appropriate discussions: Engage your children in age-appropriate discussions about money, teaching them the value of financial responsibility. Help them understand the importance of saving, budgeting and making conscious choices with their money.

Setting boundaries: Teach your children about financial boundaries, helping them understand the difference between wants and needs. By instilling healthy financial habits, you empower them to make wise choices and avoid unnecessary debt or financial stress.

CULTIVATING GRATITUDE FOR ABUNDANCE

Gratitude practices: Introduce gratitude practices into your daily routine as a family. Encourage your children to express gratitude for the abundance in their lives, whether it's material possessions, experiences, relationships or personal growth.

Abundance affirmations: Teach your children affirmations that reinforce the mindset of abundance and prosperity. Encourage them to repeat affirmations such as, 'I am grateful for the abundance in my life,' or, 'I attract prosperity and abundance with gratitude.'

VALUING EXPERIENCES OVER POSSESSIONS

Experiential gifts: Emphasise the value of experiences over material possessions by gifting your children with experiences like outings, adventures or quality time together. Teach them that memories and shared moments hold more significance and fulfilment than mere possessions.

Exposing to diverse experiences: Expose your children to a variety of experiences, cultures and perspectives to broaden their understanding of abundance. Teach them to appreciate the richness of life in its many forms, rather than equating abundance solely with material wealth.

GIVING BACK AND SHARING ABUNDANCE

Acts of kindness: Engage your children in acts of kindness and generosity, such as donating to charity, volunteering or helping those in need. Teach them that sharing their abundance with others not only benefits those in need but also amplifies their own sense of abundance.

Sharing resources: Encourage your children to share their resources with others, whether it's toys, clothes or food. Teach them the value of generosity and how sharing can create a cycle of abundance that benefits everyone involved.

Living in abundance goes beyond mere financial wealth; it encompasses a mindset of gratitude, appreciation and generosity. By teaching our children about financial responsibility, cultivating gratitude for the abundance in their lives, valuing experiences over possessions and sharing their abundance with others, we empower them to attract prosperity and abundance in all areas of life. Let your children know that abundance is not about lack or excessive material possessions, but about a mindset of gratitude and appreciation for all the blessings life has to offer. Embrace the joy of living in abundance and guide your children to do the same, knowing that true wealth lies in the richness of experiences, relationships and the love that surrounds them.

By embracing gratitude, moms can shift their perspective, cultivate a positive mindset and effortlessly manifest their desires.

GRATITUDE AS A LIFE HACK

Reconnecting busy moms with the flow of manifesting

In the hustle and bustle of motherhood, finding balance and staying connected to the flow of manifesting can sometimes feel like an uphill battle. However, gratitude offers a powerful life hack that busy moms can utilse to reconnect with the flow and align themselves with the abundant universe. By embracing gratitude, moms can shift their perspective, cultivate a positive mindset and effortlessly manifest their desires.

SHIFTING PERSPECTIVE THROUGH GRATITUDE

Gratitude acts as a lens through which moms can shift their perspective and see the world in a more positive light. It helps them focus on the blessings, joys and abundance that surround them, even amidst the chaos of their busy lives. By consciously choosing to appreciate the small moments of beauty, the acts of kindness and the love that fills their days, moms reframe their experiences and invite more positivity into their lives. Shifting perspective through gratitude becomes a powerful tool to reconnect with the flow of manifesting.

CULTIVATING A POSITIVE MINDSET

Gratitude is a gateway to cultivating a positive mindset. Busy moms who practice gratitude regularly train their minds to seek out the good in every situation. They become aware of their thoughts and intentionally redirect their attention to the aspects of their lives that bring them joy, fulfilment and abundance. A positive mindset opens up space for new possibilities, attracts positive experiences and aligns moms with the flow of manifesting effortlessly.

HARNESSING THE POWER OF VIBRATIONAL ENERGY

Gratitude operates on the principle that like attracts like. When moms express gratitude for the blessings in their lives, they raise their vibrational energy and emit a frequency that is in alignment with the abundant universe. This higher vibration acts as a magnet, attracting more blessings, opportunities and positive experiences. Busy moms who harness the power of vibrational energy through gratitude find themselves effortlessly flowing with the rhythm of manifesting.

CREATING AN ABUNDANCE MINDSET

Gratitude is a key ingredient in cultivating an abundance mindset. By acknowledging and appreciating what they already have, moms shift their focus from scarcity to abundance. They recognise that there is always more to be grateful for and that the universe is infinitely abundant. With an abundance mindset, moms tap into a limitless well of possibilities, expanding their capacity to manifest their desires and attract more abundance into their lives.

MANIFESTING FROM A STATE OF ALIGNMENT

Gratitude helps busy moms align themselves with the flow of manifesting. When moms express sincere gratitude, they align their thoughts, emotions and actions with their desires. They release resistance, let go of limiting beliefs and surrender control, allowing the universe to orchestrate the perfect alignment of circumstances for their manifestations to unfold. By manifesting from a state of alignment, busy moms effortlessly attract what they desire into their lives.

PRACTICING GRATITUDE RITUALS

To make gratitude a daily habit, busy moms can incorporate gratitude rituals into their routines. They can start their mornings by journalling three things they are grateful for, recite affirmations of gratitude throughout the day or create a gratitude jar where they collect notes of appreciation. These rituals serve as gentle reminders to stay connected to the flow of manifesting, even in the midst of their busy schedules.

SHARING GRATITUDE WITH OTHERS

Gratitude becomes even more powerful when it is shared with others. Busy moms can cultivate a culture of gratitude within their families by expressing appreciation for one another and encouraging their children to do the same. They can also extend their gratitude to friends, colleagues and the broader community through acts of kindness and appreciation. By sharing gratitude, busy moms not only uplift others but also create a ripple effect of positivity and abundance.

Gratitude serves as a life hack for busy moms to reconnect with the flow of manifesting. By shifting their perspective and utilising the life hack of gratitude, anything is possible.

Forgiveness

By cultivating empathy and compassion through forgiveness, moms and their children create a more harmonious and virtuous family dynamic.

THE POWER OF FORGIVENESS

Creating freedom and virtue in the lives of moms and children

Forgiveness is a transformative act of liberation that holds the power to heal wounds, release burdens and cultivate a life of freedom and virtue. By learning how to forgive and showing their children a healthy relationship with forgiveness, moms create a nurturing environment that fosters emotional wellbeing, strengthens relationships and paves the way for a more virtuous and fulfilling life.

UNDERSTANDING THE ESSENCE OF FORGIVENESS

Forgiveness is a profound act of compassion and understanding. It involves letting go of resentment, anger and the desire for revenge. When moms embrace forgiveness, they free themselves from the shackles of negative emotions, allowing healing and growth to take place. Forgiveness is not about condoning hurtful actions but about choosing to release the emotional baggage that weighs them down.

HEALING EMOTIONAL WOUNDS

Forgiveness is a powerful tool for healing emotional wounds, both for moms and their children. By forgiving past hurts, moms release the emotional pain that lingers within them, allowing for personal healing and growth. They create space for positive emotions, such as love, compassion and joy, to flourish. Teaching their children the value of forgiveness empowers them to navigate conflicts and heal their own emotional wounds, fostering emotional resilience and wellbeing.

STRENGTHENING RELATIONSHIPS

Forgiveness plays a vital role in strengthening relationships, fostering deeper connections and promoting harmony within the family. By forgiving one another, moms and their children create an environment of trust, understanding and acceptance. Forgiveness opens the door to honest communication, empathy and the resolution of conflicts. It allows for the restoration of damaged relationships and the cultivation of healthier, more loving connections.

MODELLING HEALTHY EMOTIONAL EXPRESSION

As moms learn to forgive, they model healthy emotional expression for their children. By openly discussing their feelings, acknowledging the pain caused and choosing forgiveness, moms demonstrate the power of vulnerability, empathy and emotional growth. Children learn that it is okay to experience a range of emotions and that forgiveness is a strength rather than a weakness. This modelling encourages children to develop their own healthy emotional expression and conflict resolution skills.

CULTIVATING EMPATHY AND COMPASSION

Forgiveness is rooted in empathy and compassion. When moms forgive, they put themselves in the shoes of the person who caused the hurt, seeking to understand their perspectives and motivations. This empathy and compassion extend not only to others but also to themselves. Moms learn to forgive themselves for their own perceived shortcomings and mistakes, fostering self-compassion and self-growth. By cultivating empathy and compassion through forgiveness, moms and their children create a more harmonious and virtuous family dynamic.

PROMOTING A VIRTUOUS LIFE

Forgiveness is an integral part of leading a virtuous life. By practicing forgiveness, moms and their children embrace virtues such as compassion, empathy, humility and resilience. They learn to let go of grudges, promote understanding and seek solutions that honour the wellbeing of all involved. Forgiveness becomes a cornerstone of their character, guiding them in their interactions with others and in their personal growth.

LIVING A FREE-FLOWING LIFE

The act of forgiveness frees moms and their children from the burden of carrying past hurts. It allows them to live a free-flowing life, unencumbered by resentments and bitterness. Moms who forgive create space for more joy, love, and positive experiences in their lives. They teach their children that holding onto grudges hinders personal growth and limits one's ability to fully embrace life's blessings. Forgiveness becomes a pathway to living a life filled with freedom, authenticity and inner peace.

By embracing forgiveness and demonstrating its importance to their children, moms create an environment that nurtures emotional wellbeing, strengthens relationships and lays the foundation for a positive future.

THE ART OF FORGIVENESS

Healing and moving forward as a mom

Motherhood is a journey of love, growth and connection, but it is also a path that presents its fair share of challenges, conflicts and misunderstandings. As moms, we strive to create a harmonious and loving environment for our children, but sometimes, we find ourselves facing situations that require the art of forgiveness. In this chapter, we explore the profound power of forgiveness, how it can heal our hearts and how it enables us to move forward with grace and compassion on our journey of motherhood.

UNDERSTANDING FORGIVENESS

Forgiveness is a transformative process that involves letting go of resentment, anger and the desire for revenge. It is not about condoning or forgetting the actions that caused pain, but rather a conscious choice to release ourselves from the emotional burden that holds us back. Forgiveness allows us to reclaim our power, heal our hearts and create space for healing, growth and positive change.

HEALING OUR HEARTS

Holding onto grudges and resentments weighs heavily on our hearts and affects our overall wellbeing. Forgiveness offers us the opportunity to heal and free ourselves from the emotional pain that lingers within. By forgiving, we release negative energy and open ourselves up to love, compassion and inner peace. It is a process of reclaiming our power and taking back control of our emotional state.

CULTIVATING COMPASSION AND EMPATHY

Forgiveness is rooted in compassion and empathy. It requires us to put ourselves in the shoes of others, recognising their humanness, flaws and vulnerabilities. By cultivating empathy, we gain a deeper understanding of the circumstances and perspectives that led to the hurtful actions. This understanding does not justify the actions, but it allows us to find compassion in our hearts and see the potential for growth and change.

FORGIVING OURSELVES

As moms, we often hold ourselves to high standards and may feel guilty or inadequate when we make mistakes. Forgiving ourselves is an essential part of the healing process. We are human, and we will inevitably make errors along the way. Embracing self-forgiveness allows us to let go of self-blame and shame, opening ourselves up to self-love and growth. It is an act of acknowledging our imperfections and embracing our journey with compassion and acceptance.

REBUILDING TRUST AND CONNECTION

Forgiveness can be a catalyst for rebuilding trust and strengthening connections in our relationships. It offers an opportunity for open communication, vulnerability and growth. By extending forgiveness, we create a safe space for healing and reestablishing bonds of love and trust. It is a chance to move forward together, with a renewed commitment to understanding, empathy and mutual respect.

TEACHING FORGIVENESS TO OUR CHILDREN

As moms, we have a profound influence on our children's emotional development. Teaching them the art of forgiveness is a valuable life lesson. By modelling forgiveness in our own lives, we show them the importance of empathy, compassion and emotional intelligence. We guide them towards understanding that forgiveness is not a sign of weakness, but a strength that allows us to let go of pain and create harmonious relationships. Through open conversations and age-appropriate explanations, we can help our children navigate conflicts and teach them the art of forgiveness.

MOVING FORWARD WITH GRACE

Forgiveness is a transformative process that enables us to move forward with grace and resilience. It liberates us from the shackles of the past, freeing up mental and emotional space for new experiences and growth. By embracing forgiveness, we release the weight of resentment and create a pathway towards a more peaceful and fulfilling future. It allows us to focus on the present moment, nurture our relationships and make choices that align with our values and aspirations as mothers.

The art of forgiveness is a profound tool for healing, growth and moving forward as a mom. It enables us to heal our hearts, cultivate compassion and understanding, forgive ourselves, rebuild trust, teach forgiveness to our children and embrace the transformative power of letting go. By embracing forgiveness in our lives, we create a nurturing environment for ourselves and our families, fostering love, peace and growth on our journey of motherhood.

Engage in forgiveness journalling, where we write letters of forgiveness to ourselves or those who have hurt us. This practice allows us to release emotions, gain clarity and foster healing.

THE GIFT OF FORGIVENESS

Fostering emotional freedom for yourself and your children

Forgiveness is a transformative and healing practice that holds immense power for both moms and their children. As moms, we have the opportunity to model and teach the gift of forgiveness, allowing ourselves and our children to experience emotional freedom and release the burdens of resentment and hurt. In this chapter, we delve into the profound impact of forgiveness, explore forgiveness practices and discover how it nurtures the wellbeing and growth of both ourselves and our children.

UNDERSTANDING FORGIVENESS

The nature of forgiveness: Explore the essence of forgiveness, which is the conscious choice to release negative feelings, resentment and the desire for revenge. Understand that forgiveness does not condone hurtful actions but rather empowers us to heal and move forward.

BENEFITS OF FORGIVENESS

Emotional liberation: Discover how forgiveness frees us from the emotional baggage that weighs us down, fostering emotional wellbeing and allowing us to live with greater peace and joy.

Healing and transformation: Learn how forgiveness contributes to our personal growth and transformation, opening the doors for healing and creating space for new beginnings.

Improved relationships: Understand how forgiveness nurtures healthier and more authentic connections with our children and others, fostering trust, empathy and compassion.

SELF-FORGIVENESS

Embracing self-compassion: Recognise the importance of self-forgiveness in our own personal growth as moms. Release self-judgement and cultivate self-compassion, understanding that we are human and make mistakes.

Releasing guilt and shame: Learn forgiveness practices that help us release guilt and shame associated with perceived shortcomings as moms. Embrace the understanding that we are doing our best with the resources and knowledge we have.

TEACHING FORGIVENESS TO CHILDREN

Modelling forgiveness: Understand the influential role we play as moms in modelling forgiveness for our children. Embrace forgiveness in our interactions with them and others, demonstrating the power of letting go and fostering emotional wellbeing.

Cultivating empathy and understanding: Teach our children the importance of empathy and understanding towards others, helping them develop the capacity for forgiveness and compassion.

FORGIVENESS PRACTICES

Journalling: Engage in forgiveness journalling, where we write letters of forgiveness to ourselves or those who have hurt us. This practice allows us to release emotions, gain clarity and foster healing.

Meditation and visualisation: Utilise forgiveness meditation and visualisation techniques to cultivate a state of inner peace and compassion, extending forgiveness to ourselves and others.

Affirmations: Practice forgiveness affirmations, repeating statements that affirm our intention to forgive and let go of resentments. Affirmations help reframe our mindset and create positive shifts.

THE JOURNEY OF FORGIVENESS

Patience and time: Understand that forgiveness is a process and that it may take time to fully release and heal. Embrace patience and kindness towards ourselves and our children as we navigate the journey of forgiveness.

Seeking support: Seek support from trusted friends, mentors or therapists to guide us through the forgiveness process, providing us with insights, perspective and emotional support.

The gift of forgiveness is a profound and liberating practice that brings emotional freedom and healing to both ourselves and our children. By embracing forgiveness, we release the burdens of resentment, foster emotional wellbeing, and cultivate deeper connections. Let us embark on the transformative journey of forgiveness, gifting ourselves and our children the invaluable freedom to thrive and live with love, compassion and emotional liberation.

As mothers, we often hold ourselves to high standards and can be our own harshest critics. Practicing self-forgiveness is crucial for our wellbeing and sets an example of self-love and acceptance for our children.

THE FREEDOM OF
FORGIVENESS

*Cultivating emotional resilience
for yourself and your children*

In the journey of motherhood, forgiveness is a powerful tool that can liberate us from the burdens of the past and create emotional resilience for both ourselves and our children. By embracing forgiveness, we open ourselves to healing, growth and the freedom to live a more joyful and fulfilled life. In this chapter, we delve into the transformative power of forgiveness, exploring how it can cultivate emotional resilience and create a positive environment for ourselves and our children.

UNDERSTANDING THE HEALING POWER OF FORGIVENESS

Releasing emotional baggage: Forgiveness allows us to let go of anger, resentment and pain that can weigh us down. By releasing emotional baggage, we create space for healing and emotional wellbeing.

Breaking the cycle: Forgiveness breaks the cycle of hurt and negativity, preventing it from passing on to our children. It frees us from perpetuating patterns of pain and allows us to create a healthier, more loving environment for our family.

PRACTICING SELF-FORGIVENESS

Embracing self-compassion: As mothers, we often hold ourselves to high standards and can be our own harshest critics. Practicing self-forgiveness is crucial for our wellbeing and sets an example of self-love and acceptance for our children.

Letting go of guilt: Forgiving ourselves for past mistakes or perceived shortcomings is essential for our personal growth and happiness. It allows us to move forward with a renewed sense of purpose and self-worth.

TEACHING FORGIVENESS TO OUR CHILDREN

Modelling forgiveness: Our children learn from observing our actions and attitudes. By modelling forgiveness in our own lives, we teach them the importance of forgiveness and offer them a framework for resolving conflicts and fostering healthy relationships.

Empathy and understanding: Encourage empathy and understanding in your children by teaching them to put themselves in others' shoes. Help them recognise that forgiveness is an act of compassion and strength that can lead to healing and connection.

THE PROCESS OF FORGIVENESS

Acknowledging and processing emotions: Forgiveness does not mean suppressing or denying our emotions. It involves acknowledging and processing the pain, anger or resentment we may feel. Support your children in expressing their emotions in a healthy and constructive manner.

Releasing attachments to the past: Forgiveness is a process of letting go of attachments to past grievances. Teach your children that holding onto grudges or seeking revenge only perpetuates pain and blocks personal growth.

THE GIFT OF EMOTIONAL FREEDOM

Cultivating emotional resilience: Forgiveness cultivates emotional resilience by teaching us to navigate challenging emotions and situations with grace and compassion. Help your children understand that forgiveness is a tool for their own wellbeing and growth.

Creating harmonious relationships: By fostering forgiveness within our family dynamics, we create an atmosphere of trust, love and understanding. It promotes healthier communication, conflict resolution and deeper connections among family members.

Forgiveness is a powerful and transformative practice that frees us from the burdens of the past, cultivates emotional resilience and creates a harmonious environment for ourselves and our children. By embracing forgiveness, both for ourselves and others, we create a foundation of emotional wellbeing and teach our children the value of compassion, empathy and personal growth. Through forgiveness, we break the chains of resentment and create a future filled with love, understanding and emotional freedom for ourselves and our children. Embrace the transformative power of forgiveness and embark on a journey of healing and resilience, knowing that by forgiving, we open ourselves to a life of greater joy, peace and fulfilment.

*Forgiveness is an opportunity for personal growth
and resilience.*

THE HEALING POWER OF FORGIVENESS

Liberating yourself and your children

Forgiveness is a transformative and liberating act that holds immense power to heal emotional wounds and restore inner peace. As mothers, cultivating forgiveness within ourselves and teaching it to our children is a gift that can positively shape their lives. In this chapter, we explore the healing power of forgiveness and how it can bring liberation and emotional wellbeing to both ourselves and our children. By embracing forgiveness, we create a foundation of love, compassion and growth within our families.

UNDERSTANDING THE NATURE OF FORGIVENESS

Letting go of resentment: Forgiveness involves releasing resentment, anger and the desire for revenge. It is a conscious choice to free ourselves from the emotional burdens that hold us back.

Embracing compassion and empathy: Forgiveness is an act of compassion and empathy, where we strive to understand the perspectives and struggles of others, including our children. It opens the door for healing and growth.

THE HEALING BENEFITS OF FORGIVENESS

Emotional liberation: Forgiveness liberates us from the shackles of negative emotions, allowing us to experience emotional freedom and inner peace. It frees up energy that can be redirected towards positive growth.

Strengthening relationships: Forgiveness has the power to repair and strengthen relationships. It fosters understanding, empathy and the willingness to work through challenges, creating deeper connections with our children.

Personal growth and resilience: Forgiveness is an opportunity for personal growth and resilience. It allows us to learn from experiences, cultivate empathy and develop emotional strength. By modelling forgiveness, we teach our children important life skills.

PRACTICING FORGIVENESS

Self-forgiveness: Begin by forgiving yourself for any perceived shortcomings or mistakes. Recognise that we are all imperfect beings on a journey of growth and learning. Embrace self-compassion and allow yourself to heal and grow.

Communicating openly: Encourage open and honest communication with your children. Create a safe space where they can express their feelings and experiences without fear of judgement. Teach them to voice their emotions and seek resolution through forgiveness.

Teaching empathy and understanding: Help your children develop empathy and understanding towards others. Teach them the value of putting themselves in someone else's shoes and seeking forgiveness when they have hurt someone.

THE PROCESS OF FORGIVENESS

Acknowledging and processing emotions: Allow yourself and your children to acknowledge and process the emotions that arise from hurtful experiences. Validate their feelings and guide them through healthy ways of expressing and understanding those emotions.

Choosing forgiveness: Encourage the act of choosing forgiveness as a conscious decision to let go of resentment and create space for healing. Emphasise that forgiveness is not about condoning harmful actions but about freeing ourselves from the burden of anger and resentment.

Embracing healing rituals: Engage in healing rituals, such as writing forgiveness letters, practicing meditation or mindfulness or seeking professional support if needed. These rituals can support the process of forgiveness and provide a path to emotional healing.

THE GIFT OF FORGIVENESS

Cultivating gratitude: Forgiveness opens the door to gratitude and appreciation. Encourage your children to find gratitude for the lessons learned, personal growth, and the opportunity to create more loving and harmonious relationships.

Embracing a future of love and compassion: Forgiveness creates a future filled with love and compassion. It allows us to break free from the cycles of pain and hurt, creating a legacy of forgiveness and emotional wellbeing for our children and future generations.

The healing power of forgiveness is a profound gift that can liberate ourselves and our children from emotional burdens and bring forth love, compassion and growth. By embracing forgiveness, we create a nurturing environment where healing and personal growth can flourish. Through open communication, practicing empathy and teaching the value of forgiveness, we instil in our children the ability to navigate challenges with resilience and create deep, meaningful connections. Remember, forgiveness is a journey, and as mothers, we have the power to guide our children towards emotional liberation and a future filled with love and compassion.

Cultivating trust in yourself, your children and the process of motherhood allows you to navigate with confidence and grace.

SURRENDER AND TRUST

Finding peace in the flow of motherhood

Motherhood is a journey that often requires us to navigate through unexpected twists and turns, challenges and uncertainties. Amidst the chaos, finding peace and maintaining a sense of balance can feel like an elusive goal. In this chapter, we explore the concepts of surrender and trust as powerful tools for finding peace in the flow of motherhood. By embracing these principles, we can release control, let go of unrealistic expectations and cultivate a deep sense of trust in ourselves, our children and the journey of motherhood.

EMBRACING SURRENDER

Letting go of control: Understand that not everything is within your control, and trying to micromanage every aspect of motherhood can lead to unnecessary stress and frustration. Surrendering control allows you to be more present, adaptable and open to the natural flow of life.

Embracing imperfections: Accept that perfection is unattainable and that mistakes and imperfections are part of the journey. Embrace the beauty in imperfection and allow yourself and your children to learn and grow through trial and error.

Releasing expectations: Recognise and release any rigid expectations you may have about how motherhood should look or how your children should behave. Instead, embrace the uniqueness of your journey and your children's individuality, allowing for flexibility and growth.

CULTIVATING TRUST

Trusting your intuition: Tap into your innate wisdom and trust your intuition as a guiding force in motherhood. Develop a deep connection with your inner knowing and allow it to guide your decisions and actions.

Trusting your children: Believe in the inherent wisdom and abilities of your children. Trust that they have their own journey and lessons to learn. Provide them with a safe space to explore, make mistakes and grow into their true selves.

Trusting the process: Have faith in the journey of motherhood. Trust that even in the most challenging moments, there is a greater purpose and growth unfolding. Trust that everything is unfolding as it should and that you have the strength and resources to navigate any situation.

FINDING PEACE IN THE FLOW

Cultivating presence: Practice mindfulness and being fully present in the moment. When we are present, we can better connect with ourselves and our children, and we can respond to situations with clarity and grace.

Practicing self-care: Prioritise self-care to nourish your mind, body and spirit. When you take care of yourself, you replenish your energy reserves and create a foundation of peace and wellbeing from which you can parent more effectively.

Celebrating small joys: Cultivate gratitude and appreciation for the small moments of joy and beauty in everyday life. By noticing and savouring these moments, you can shift your focus from challenges to the abundance of blessings that surround you.

Surrendering and trusting in the journey of motherhood can be transformative, allowing you to find peace, joy and fulfilment amidst the ups and downs. By embracing surrender, you release the need for control and perfection, embracing imperfection and growth instead. Cultivating trust in yourself, your children and the process of motherhood allows you to navigate with confidence and grace. As you surrender and trust, you find yourself flowing effortlessly with the currents of motherhood, experiencing a profound sense of peace, connection and love. Embrace surrender and trust as your guiding principles, and watch as the magic of motherhood unfolds in beautiful and unexpected ways.

Belief

When moms believe in themselves, they lead by example, demonstrating to their children the importance of self-belief.

THE BEAUTY OF SELF-BELIEF

Empowering moms and inspiring transformation

When moms believe in themselves as much as they believe in their children, a profound beauty emerges in their lives. This self-belief becomes a catalyst for personal growth, empowerment and the ability to create positive change. By recognising their own worth and potential, moms unlock a wellspring of beauty that influences their actions and transforms their journey of motherhood.

RECOGNISING INNER STRENGTH AND POTENTIAL

Self-belief is rooted in recognising one's inner strength and potential. Moms who believe in themselves understand that they possess unique talents, abilities and qualities that contribute to their role as mothers and as individuals. They acknowledge their capacity to make a difference and trust in their ability to navigate the challenges of motherhood. Recognising their inner strength and potential allows moms to tap into a well of confidence and resilience.

LEADING BY EXAMPLE

When moms believe in themselves, they lead by example, demonstrating to their children the importance of self-belief. By showcasing their own self-assurance, moms inspire their children to embrace their own worth and potential. They encourage their children to dream big, pursue their passions and believe in their ability to achieve their goals. Leading by example, moms become powerful role models who empower their children to believe in themselves.

EMBRACING GROWTH AND PERSONAL DEVELOPMENT

Self-belief opens the door to growth and personal development. Moms who believe in themselves are open to new experiences, willing to step out of their comfort zones and committed to continuous learning. They embrace challenges as opportunities for growth and view setbacks as valuable lessons. By prioritising their personal development, moms expand their knowledge, skills and perspectives, enhancing their ability to navigate the complexities of motherhood.

FOSTERING RESILIENCE AND PERSEVERANCE

Self-belief nurtures resilience and perseverance in the face of adversity. Moms who believe in themselves possess an unwavering belief that they can overcome obstacles and rise above challenges. They view setbacks as temporary roadblocks rather than permanent barriers. Fuelled by their self-belief, moms demonstrate resilience, bouncing back from setbacks with determination and perseverance. Their ability to navigate challenges with grace and tenacity inspires their children to develop their own resilience.

CULTIVATING SELF-CARE AND WELLBEING

Self-belief is intimately connected to self-care and wellbeing. Moms who believe in themselves prioritise their own physical, emotional and mental wellbeing. They understand that caring for themselves allows them to show up fully for their children and loved ones. By making self-care a priority, moms nourish their own sense of self-worth and reinforce their belief in themselves. This cultivation of self-care and wellbeing becomes a foundation for a balanced and fulfilling motherhood journey.

EMBODYING AUTHENTICITY AND CONFIDENCE

Self-belief empowers moms to embrace their authenticity and exude confidence. When moms believe in themselves, they trust in their instincts, values and choices. They have the courage to be true to themselves and make decisions aligned with their authentic selves. This authenticity and confidence radiate from within, positively impacting their relationships and inspiring others to believe in themselves as well.

CREATING POSITIVE CHANGE AND IMPACT

The beauty of self-belief lies in its ability to create positive change and impact. Moms who believe in themselves are more likely to take courageous actions, challenge societal norms and advocate for positive change. They recognise their power to make a difference not only in their own lives but also in the lives of their children and the broader community. By believing in themselves, moms become agents of transformation, spreading beauty and inspiring others to believe in themselves too.

As moms believe in themselves as much as they believe in their children, they unlock a beauty within that influences their actions, fosters personal growth and inspires transformation.

When a mother wholeheartedly believes in her child, she bestows upon them a gift of immeasurable value – a sense of worth, confidence and a foundation of self-belief.

MOTHER'S BELIEF IN THEIR CHILD

Foundation of golden possibilities

In the vast realm of motherhood, there exists a profound and transformative power that holds the potential to shape the destiny of a child. It is the unwavering belief that a mother holds in her child, a golden foundation of possibilities. This chapter delves into the extraordinary significance of a mother's belief, exploring how it serves as a catalyst for growth, resilience and limitless potential in her child's life.

THE POWER OF BELIEF

Belief is a force that transcends limitations, defies odds and unlocks hidden potentials. When a mother wholeheartedly believes in her child, she bestows upon them a gift of immeasurable value — a sense of worth, confidence and a foundation of self-belief. This belief becomes a guiding light, illuminating the path of a child's journey, instilling within them the courage to dream, persevere and achieve greatness.

NURTURING SELF-WORTH

A mother's belief in her child nurtures a profound sense of self-worth. When a child feels unconditionally accepted and valued by their mother, they develop a solid foundation of self-esteem. This sense of worthiness becomes a protective shield, allowing the child to face life's challenges with resilience, knowing that they are deserving of love, success and happiness.

UNLEASHING POTENTIAL

A mother's belief holds the key to unlocking her child's hidden potential. When a mother sees her child's unique strengths, talents and abilities, she becomes a catalyst for their growth and development. By fostering an environment that encourages exploration and self-expression, a mother empowers her child to step into their authentic selves, embrace their passions and pursue their dreams fearlessly.

OVERCOMING OBSTACLES

Belief is a powerful tool that enables a child to overcome obstacles and adversity. When a mother believes in her child's ability to overcome challenges, she instils within them a sense of resilience, determination and a refusal to be defined by setbacks. This unwavering belief becomes a guiding force that propels the child forward, even in the face of adversity, teaching them invaluable life lessons and instilling within them an unwavering spirit.

FUELLING AMBITION

A mother's belief fuels her child's ambition and thirst for success. When a child feels supported, encouraged and believed in by their mother, they develop a deep-seated drive to pursue their passions and goals. A mother's belief serves as a constant reminder that the sky is the limit, instilling in her child the confidence to reach for the stars and create a life of purpose and fulfilment.

PRACTICAL APPLICATIONS OF BELIEF

Unconditional acceptance: A mother can cultivate belief by unconditionally accepting and loving her child, embracing their uniqueness and celebrating their individuality. By creating an environment of acceptance and non-judgement, a mother instils in her child a sense of self-worth and empowers them to embrace their authentic selves.

Encouragement and affirmation: A mother can actively nurture belief by offering genuine encouragement and affirmation. By acknowledging and celebrating her child's accomplishments, both big and small, a mother reinforces their belief in themselves and their abilities.

Setting high expectations: A mother can set high expectations for her child, challenging them to reach their full potential. By communicating her belief in their ability to succeed, a mother motivates her child to strive for excellence and surpass their own expectations.

Embracing growth mindset: A mother can foster belief by cultivating a growth mindset in herself and her child. By emphasising the power of effort, resilience and continuous learning, a mother encourages her child to see challenges as opportunities for growth and development.

A mother's belief in her child is a foundational gold, a transformative force that nurtures self-worth, unleashes potential and fuels ambition. With this belief, a mother empowers her child to embrace their uniqueness, overcome obstacles and reach for their dreams. As mothers harness the power of belief, they shape the future, instilling within their children a sense of limitless possibilities and a firm foundation to navigate the world with confidence, purpose and resilience.

By harnessing the power of empowering beliefs, we can tap into our full potential and create a meaningful and fulfilling motherhood journey.

EMPOWERING BELIEFS

Unleashing your potential as a mother

As mothers, we hold within us the incredible power to shape the lives of our children and create a nurturing environment for their growth and development. However, to fully step into our role as empowered mothers, we must cultivate empowering beliefs that unleash our own potential. In this chapter, we explore the transformative impact of empowering beliefs and how they can elevate our experience of motherhood, enabling us to embrace our strengths, overcome challenges and create a positive impact on our children and ourselves.

THE POWER OF BELIEFS

Beliefs are the lenses through which we perceive ourselves and the world around us. They shape our thoughts, emotions and actions, influencing the choices we make and the outcomes we experience. Empowering beliefs are those that support our growth, self-worth and ability to thrive as mothers. By harnessing the power of empowering beliefs, we can tap into our full potential and create a meaningful and fulfilling motherhood journey.

IDENTIFYING LIMITING BELIEFS

Before we can embrace empowering beliefs, it is essential to identify and challenge any limiting beliefs that may be holding us back. These are the beliefs that undermine our confidence, create self-doubt and hinder our ability to fully embrace our role as mothers. By becoming aware of these limiting beliefs, we can examine their origins, question their validity and consciously choose to let go of them, making space for empowering beliefs to take their place.

CULTIVATING EMPOWERING BELIEFS

Cultivating empowering beliefs requires a conscious effort and a commitment to our growth as mothers. It starts with recognising our strengths, talents and innate wisdom. We can choose to believe in our abilities to navigate the challenges of motherhood, make wise decisions and create a loving and supportive environment for our children. Empowering beliefs may include affirmations such as, 'I am a capable and loving mother,' 'I trust my instincts,' and, 'I embrace the journey of motherhood with confidence and grace.'

HARNESSING THE POWER OF VISUALISATION AND AFFIRMATIONS

Visualisation and affirmations are powerful tools for reinforcing empowering beliefs. By visualising ourselves embodying the qualities we desire as mothers and affirming positive statements, we reprogram our subconscious mind and align our thoughts and actions with our empowering beliefs. These practices help us build confidence, overcome self-doubt and tap into our inner strength, enabling us to show up as the best versions of ourselves for our children.

TRANSFORMING CHALLENGES INTO OPPORTUNITIES

Empowering beliefs empower us to transform challenges into opportunities for growth and learning. Instead of seeing setbacks or difficulties as obstacles, we can choose to view them as stepping stones to personal and maternal development. Empowering beliefs allow us to reframe our experiences, embrace resilience and approach challenges with a mindset of curiosity and growth. They remind us that we have the inner resources and strength to navigate any situation that arises.

LEADING BY EXAMPLE

As mothers, our beliefs have a profound impact on our children. By embodying empowering beliefs, we become powerful role models, demonstrating the importance of self-belief, resilience and a positive mindset. Our children absorb our energy and beliefs, so it is essential to lead by example and show them what is possible when we believe in ourselves and embrace our potential.

Empowering beliefs have the potential to transform our experience of motherhood and unleash our full potential as mothers. By identifying and challenging limiting beliefs, cultivating empowering beliefs, harnessing the power of visualisation and affirmations and transforming challenges into opportunities, we can create a nurturing and empowering environment for ourselves and our children. As we embrace empowering beliefs, we elevate our experience of motherhood and inspire our children to believe in themselves and their own potential. Let us embrace the power of empowering beliefs and unleash the incredible potential within us as mothers.

Release the habit of comparing yourself to other moms. Embrace the understanding that each mother's journey is unique, and your worth is not diminished by the accomplishments or choices of others.

EMPOWERING BELIEFS FOR MOMS

Embracing your worth and strengths

As moms, we often find ourselves questioning our worth and doubting our abilities. However, it is essential to recognise that we possess inherent worth and strengths that make us extraordinary caregivers and role models for our children. In this chapter, we explore empowering beliefs that uplift and empower moms, helping them embrace their worth, tap into their strengths and navigate motherhood with confidence and self-assurance.

BELIEF IN SELF-WORTH

Recognising your value: Understand that you are inherently worthy, deserving of love, respect and self-care. Embrace the belief that your worth as a mom is not dependent on external validation or perfection.

Letting go of comparison: Release the habit of comparing yourself to other moms. Embrace the understanding that each mother's journey is unique, and your worth is not diminished by the accomplishments or choices of others.

STRENGTHS AND ABILITIES

Celebrating your strengths: Identify and celebrate your unique strengths as a mom. Acknowledge the qualities that make you an exceptional caregiver and role model for your children.

Embracing your intuition: Trust your intuition and maternal instincts. Recognise the inherent wisdom within you, guiding you to make the best decisions for your children and family.

EMBRACING IMPERFECTIONS

Embracing imperfection: Understand that perfection is an illusion. Embrace the beauty in your imperfections and recognise that they make you relatable, authentic and human.

Learning from mistakes: See mistakes as opportunities for growth and learning. Embrace the belief that your worth is not diminished by the errors you make but rather by your ability to learn, evolve and persevere.

SELF-CARE AND SELF-COMPASSION

Prioritising self-care: Believe that self-care is not selfish but necessary for your wellbeing and effectiveness as a mom. Prioritise activities that recharge and nourish your body, mind and spirit.

Practicing self-compassion: Cultivate self-compassion and treat yourself with kindness and understanding. Embrace the belief that you deserve love, care and forgiveness, just like anyone else.

POSITIVE AFFIRMATIONS

Affirming your worth: Create empowering affirmations that reinforce your worth as a mom. Repeat statements such as, 'I am a loving and capable mom,' or, 'I trust my instincts and make choices that serve the wellbeing of my children.'

Challenging negative self-talk: Challenge negative self-talk and replace it with positive and empowering beliefs. Reframe self-doubt into self-assurance and embrace the belief that you are enough.

SUPPORT AND CONNECTION

Surrounding yourself with positive influences: Seek out supportive communities, friends or mentors who uplift and validate your worth as a mom. Surround yourself with those who celebrate your strengths and offer encouragement.

Building connections: Believe in the power of connecting with other moms, sharing experiences and offering support. Embrace the belief that you are not alone in your journey and that there is strength in unity.

Embracing empowering beliefs is essential for moms to cultivate self-worth, tap into their strengths and navigate motherhood with confidence and grace. By recognising your inherent worth, celebrating your strengths, embracing imperfections, prioritising self-care and surrounding yourself with positive influences, you can fully embrace your role as a mom and empower yourself to be the best version of yourself. Embrace the empowering beliefs that uplift and support you on your motherhood journey, and watch as you thrive and inspire those around you with your strength, love and resilience.

ANCHORING IN BELIEF

*Inspiring possibility and
empowerment in motherhood*

Motherhood is a journey that demands strength, resilience and unwavering belief in ourselves. Belief serves as the anchor that keeps us grounded and empowers us to navigate the challenges and uncertainties that come with raising children. In this chapter, we explore the power of belief in inspiring possibility and empowerment in motherhood. We delve into the ways in which anchoring in belief can help us overcome obstacles, tap into our inner strength and create a positive and transformative environment for ourselves and our children.

THE POWER OF BELIEF

Shaping our reality: Our beliefs shape our perception of the world and influence our actions. By anchoring in positive and empowering beliefs, we create a foundation for success, growth and personal transformation.

Overcoming challenges: Belief empowers us to overcome obstacles and face challenges with resilience and determination. It fuels our motivation and strengthens our resolve to navigate the ups and downs of motherhood.

CULTIVATING EMPOWERING BELIEFS

Self-belief and self-worth: Nurturing a deep sense of self-belief and self-worth is essential for our personal growth and the example we set for our children. Embrace affirmations and positive self-talk to reinforce empowering beliefs about yourself.

Embracing possibilities: Allow yourself to dream big and believe in the endless possibilities that lie ahead. Encourage your children to explore their passions and pursue their dreams, fostering a sense of empowerment and resilience.

CREATING AN EMPOWERING ENVIRONMENT

Positive affirmations and visualisation: Incorporate positive affirmations and visualisation techniques into your daily routine. Teach your children to use the power of positive thinking to manifest their desires and cultivate a strong belief in their capabilities.

Surrounding ourselves with support: Seek out a supportive network of like-minded individuals who share similar beliefs and values. Engage in conversations that uplift and inspire, providing a nurturing environment for growth and empowerment.

TEACHING THE POWER OF BELIEF TO OUR CHILDREN

Encouraging self-belief: Instil in your children a belief in their own abilities and strengths. Foster a growth mindset that encourages them to embrace challenges as opportunities for growth and learning.

Emphasising the power of positive thinking: Teach your children the importance of cultivating positive thoughts and beliefs. Help them understand that their beliefs shape their reality and that they have the power to create the life they desire.

OVERCOMING LIMITING BELIEFS

Identifying and challenging limiting beliefs: Explore any limiting beliefs that may be holding you back in your journey as a mother. Challenge them by examining their validity and replacing them with empowering beliefs that support your growth and wellbeing.

Supporting your children in overcoming limiting beliefs: Help your children identify and overcome their own limiting beliefs. Encourage them to challenge negative self-talk and embrace a belief in their inherent worth and potential.

EMBRACING THE POWER OF BELIEF

Embodying belief in action: Let your belief shine through your actions as a mother. Demonstrate to your children the power of belief by consistently showing up with confidence, resilience and a positive outlook on life.

Celebrating milestones and successes: Acknowledge and celebrate both your own and your children's achievements. This reinforces the belief that hard work, determination and self-belief lead to positive outcomes.

Anchoring in belief is a transformative practice that empowers us as mothers to embrace possibility, navigate challenges and create an environment of growth and empowerment for ourselves and our children. By cultivating empowering beliefs, we tap into our inner strength and inspire our children to believe in themselves and their dreams. Through belief, we transcend limitations, embrace opportunities and create a life of purpose and fulfilment. As mothers, we have the power to shape the beliefs and mindset of our children, instilling in them the confidence and resilience to overcome obstacles and pursue their passions. Embrace the power of belief, anchor yourself in possibility and watch as you and your children soar to new heights of empowerment and success in your motherhood journey.

Trusting the journey of motherhood means embracing uncertainty, growth and the transformative power it holds.

TRUSTING THE JOURNEY

Embracing uncertainty and growth in motherhood

Motherhood is a journey filled with both joys and challenges, and it is often accompanied by a sense of uncertainty. As moms, we are constantly faced with new experiences, unexpected twists and turns and the ever-changing nature of our children's lives. In this chapter, we explore the importance of trusting the journey and embracing uncertainty as a catalyst for personal growth and transformation in motherhood.

NAVIGATING THE WAVES OF UNCERTAINTY

Embracing the unknown: Recognise that uncertainty is a natural part of the motherhood journey. Embrace the idea that life is ever-evolving, and each phase brings its own unique set of opportunities and lessons.

Letting go of control: Release the need to control every aspect of your children's lives and the outcomes of your parenting efforts. Trust that by providing a loving and supportive environment, you are empowering your children to navigate their own paths.

CULTIVATING TRUST IN YOURSELF

Listening to your intuition: Tune in to your inner voice and trust your instincts as a mother. Allow your intuition to guide you in making decisions that align with your values and the unique needs of your children.

Embracing self-compassion: Offer yourself grace and kindness during moments of self-doubt. Remember that you are doing the best you can with the resources and knowledge you have. Trust that you are enough and that your love and presence are invaluable to your children.

EMBRACING GROWTH AND ADAPTATION

Embracing change as an opportunity: View life's changes and unexpected challenges as opportunities for growth, both for yourself and your children. Recognise that through adversity, resilience is built and valuable life lessons are learned.

Cultivating a growth mindset: Adopt a growth mindset, believing that you and your children have the capacity to learn, evolve and overcome obstacles. Encourage a love for learning and encourage curiosity, perseverance and a willingness to embrace new experiences.

FINDING SUPPORT AND COMMUNITY

Seeking guidance and encouragement: Surround yourself with a supportive community of fellow moms, mentors or parenting groups. Share experiences, seek advice and draw inspiration from others who are also navigating the unpredictable journey of motherhood.

Celebrating milestones and achievements: Take time to celebrate the milestones and achievements, both big and small, along your motherhood journey. Acknowledge the growth and progress made by yourself and your children, reinforcing trust in the process.

CULTIVATING RESILIENCE AND FLEXIBILITY

Embracing the power of resilience: Understand that setbacks and challenges are opportunities for resilience to flourish. Model resilience for your children, demonstrating how to bounce back from adversity and find strength in difficult times.

Remaining flexible and adaptable: Embrace flexibility and adaptability as key qualities in navigating the uncertainties of motherhood. Be open to adjusting your expectations, plans and approaches as needed, allowing for growth and new possibilities.

Trusting the journey of motherhood means embracing uncertainty, growth and the transformative power it holds. By cultivating trust in ourselves, embracing change and adaptation, seeking support, and fostering resilience, we can navigate the unpredictable nature of motherhood with grace and confidence. Trust in the process, have faith in your abilities as a mother and embrace the beauty that unfolds along the ever-unfolding journey of motherhood.

Motherhood Superpower

Finding the balance between supporting our children and allowing them to grow and learn life lessons requires empathy, understanding and resilience.

NURTURING GROWTH IN TIMES OF SICKNESS AND SELF-SABOTAGE

Motherhood brings with it the inevitable moments when our children face illness or engage in self-sabotaging behaviours. As mothers, our instinct is to protect and shield our children from pain and hardship. However, it is important to find a delicate balance between providing support and allowing them to grow and learn valuable life lessons. In this chapter, we explore strategies for nurturing growth during times of sickness and self-sabotage.

UNDERSTANDING THE NATURE OF SICKNESS

Sickness is a natural part of life, and it provides an opportunity for growth and resilience. While it is our instinct to alleviate our children's suffering, it is essential to allow them to experience and navigate illness, understanding that it is a temporary setback. By offering comfort, empathy and gentle care, we create a safe space for our children to heal while encouraging their independence and self-care.

PROMOTING SELF-REFLECTION

Self-sabotaging behaviours often arise from a lack of self-awareness or unaddressed emotional needs. During times of self-sabotage, it is important to encourage self-reflection in our children. Engage in open and non-judgemental conversations, helping them identify the underlying causes of their actions. By fostering self-awareness, we empower them to make conscious choices and take responsibility for their behavior.

TEACHING EMOTIONAL REGULATION

Emotional regulation is a crucial skill that helps our children navigate difficult emotions and make healthy choices. During times of self-sabotage, support them in recognising and understanding their emotions. Offer guidance on effective coping mechanisms, such as deep breathing, journalling or engaging in calming activities. By teaching emotional regulation, we equip them with tools to overcome self-destructive patterns and make more positive decisions.

ENCOURAGING PERSONAL RESPONSIBILITY

While providing support, it is important to encourage personal responsibility in our children's actions and decisions. Help them understand the consequences of their choices and encourage accountability. By fostering a sense of ownership, we empower them to take control of their lives and make choices aligned with their wellbeing. This allows them to grow and learn from their mistakes while building resilience.

OFFERING A SUPPORTIVE ENVIRONMENT

During times of sickness and self-sabotage, creating a supportive environment is crucial. Be a compassionate listener, allowing your children to express their fears, frustrations or anxieties without judgement. Offer encouragement and reassurance, reminding them that setbacks are opportunities for growth. Provide resources and guidance to help them seek professional help if needed, emphasising the importance of mental and physical wellbeing.

MODELLING HEALTHY BEHAVIOURS

As mothers, we play a powerful role in shaping our children's behaviour through our own actions. During times of sickness and self-sabotage, it is essential to model healthy behaviours and self-care practices. Show them how to prioritise their wellbeing by engaging in activities that promote physical, emotional and mental health. By modelling healthy behaviours, we inspire them to make positive choices for themselves.

SEEKING PROFESSIONAL SUPPORT

In some cases, seeking professional support may be necessary to help our children navigate sickness or self-sabotaging behaviours. Consult with health care professionals, therapists or counsellors who can offer expert guidance. Remember, asking for help is a sign of strength, and it shows your commitment to your child's wellbeing.

FINDING THE BALANCE

Finding the balance between supporting our children and allowing them to grow and learn life lessons requires empathy, understanding and resilience. It is a delicate dance of providing care, setting boundaries and fostering independence. By nurturing growth in times of sickness and self-sabotage, we equip our children with the tools and resilience they need to overcome challenges and thrive in their lives.

Motherhood is a profound aspect of our identity, but it does not overshadow the other dimensions of who we are.

EMBRACING IDENTITY

Enhancing the human experience of motherhood

Motherhood is a transformative journey that can bring immense joy and fulfilment. However, it is important to remember that we are not defined solely by our roles as mothers. Our identity as individuals remains an integral part of who we are, and nurturing our personal passions, dreams and interests enriches the experience of being human. In this chapter, we explore the importance of embracing our identity and allowing it to enhance our journey through motherhood.

RECOGNISING THE MULTIFACETED SELF

Motherhood is a profound aspect of our identity, but it does not overshadow the other dimensions of who we are. We have unique talents, interests and aspirations that deserve attention and cultivation. By recognising the multifaceted nature of our self, we honour the different roles we play in our lives and create a harmonious balance between our identity as mothers and as individuals.

SELF-CARE AS A PRIORITY

Taking care of our own wellbeing is not selfish; it is essential for our overall happiness and ability to be present for our children. Self-care allows us to recharge, rejuvenate and maintain a sense of self outside of motherhood. By prioritising self-care, we ensure that we have the physical, emotional and mental energy to embrace our identity fully and show up as the best version of ourselves for our children.

PURSUING PASSIONS AND INTERESTS

Motherhood should not be a barrier to pursuing our passions and interests. In fact, it can be an opportunity to integrate our personal pursuits into our role as a mother. Whether it's engaging in creative hobbies, furthering our education or pursuing career goals, allowing ourselves the space and time to pursue our passions not only enhances our sense of self but also serves as a powerful example for our children to follow their own dreams.

NURTURING RELATIONSHIPS OUTSIDE MOTHERHOOD

Maintaining meaningful relationships outside of motherhood is vital for our wellbeing. Cultivating connections with friends, partners, family members or participating in community activities provides a sense of belonging and support. These relationships offer an opportunity to engage in conversations, experiences and adventures that enrich our lives and expand our perspective beyond the realm of motherhood.

CULTIVATING MINDFULNESS AND PRESENCE

Embracing our identity requires cultivating mindfulness and presence in our daily lives. By being fully present in the moments we share with our children, we create a deep and meaningful connection. Simultaneously, we can also be present for ourselves, honouring our own needs, desires and aspirations. Mindfulness allows us to navigate the ebb and flow of motherhood while staying connected to our authentic self.

EMBRACING GROWTH AND CHANGE

Motherhood is a transformative journey that constantly challenges us to grow and adapt. Embracing our identity means embracing the growth and changes that come along with it. It is a process of self-discovery, self-reflection and embracing new possibilities. By remaining open to growth and change, we model resilience and courage for our children, showing them that embracing their own identities is a natural part of the human experience.

BUILDING A SUPPORTIVE COMMUNITY

Surrounding ourselves with a supportive community of like-minded individuals can make a significant difference in embracing our identity as mothers and individuals. Seek out other mothers who value their individuality and share similar interests or goals. Create a network of support where you can share experiences, exchange advice and uplift one another on your respective journeys.

Embracing our identity as individuals while navigating the terrain of motherhood enriches our human experience. By recognising the multifaceted nature of our self, prioritising self-care, pursuing passions, nurturing relationships outside motherhood, cultivating mindfulness, embracing growth and building a supportive community, we honour the essence of who we are and create a healthy environment for growth.

*Playfulness is not just for children; it is a gift that
we can give ourselves as mothers.*

EMBRACING THE FREE JOY OF MOTHERHOOD

Rediscovering your inner child

Motherhood is a journey filled with responsibilities, challenges and moments that require our utmost attention. However, amidst the demands of parenthood, it is crucial to remember the importance of embracing the free joy of motherhood and allowing our children to bring out our inner child. In this chapter, we explore the transformative power of having fun and reconnecting with the playful spirit within us.

THE GIFT OF PLAYFULNESS

Playfulness is not just for children; it is a gift that we can give ourselves as mothers. Engaging in playful activities with our children not only strengthens our bond but also nourishes our own wellbeing. When we allow ourselves to let go of our adult responsibilities and tap into our playful side, we create joyful memories and experiences that enrich our lives and those of our children.

RECONNECTING WITH YOUR INNER CHILD

Motherhood can sometimes lead us to forget the carefree and spontaneous nature of our own childhood. Reconnecting with our inner child involves tapping into the innocence, wonder and curiosity that we once possessed. Take time to reflect on the activities that brought you joy as a child and find ways to incorporate them into your life as a mother. Whether it's playing games, exploring nature or engaging in creative endeavours, reconnecting with your inner child opens up new possibilities for joyful experiences.

UNLEASHING CREATIVITY AND IMAGINATION

Children have a remarkable ability to see the world through the lens of creativity and imagination. As mothers, we can tap into this wellspring of creativity by participating in activities that foster imaginative play. Engage in arts and crafts, storytelling or imaginative play with your children. Embrace the freedom to think outside the box, unleash your creativity and discover new realms of joy and inspiration.

LETTING GO OF PERFECTION

The pursuit of perfection can often dampen the joy and spontaneity of motherhood. Embracing the free joy of motherhood requires letting go of the need for everything to be flawless. Give yourself permission to embrace imperfection, messy moments and spontaneous adventures. By relinquishing the need for perfection, you create space for joy, laughter and genuine connections with your children.

CREATING MAGICAL MOMENTS

Motherhood presents numerous opportunities to create magical moments with our children. Whether it's organising a themed family movie night, building forts, having a picnic in the park or simply dancing in the living room, these small gestures of joy create lasting memories for both us and our children. Embrace the power of simple pleasures and find joy in the everyday moments shared with your little ones.

CULTIVATING A SENSE OF WONDER

Children have an innate sense of wonder about the world around them. Embracing the free joy of motherhood involves cultivating our own sense of wonder and awe. Take the time to marvel at the beauty of nature, explore new places with a curious spirit and encourage your children to share their discoveries. By nurturing a sense of wonder, we foster a deep appreciation for life's small miracles and inspire our children to do the same.

FINDING BALANCE

While it is important to embrace the free joy of motherhood, it is equally important to find balance in our lives. Motherhood comes with responsibilities and obligations that cannot be ignored. Strive to strike a balance between the demands of parenthood and the need for personal joy and playfulness. By finding this equilibrium, we show our children that being a mother does not mean sacrificing our own happiness and wellbeing.

In conclusion, embracing the free joy of motherhood and reconnecting with our inner child allows us to experience the transformative power of playfulness, creativity and imagination. By letting go of perfection, creating magical moments, cultivating a sense of wonder and finding balance, we nurture a joyful and fulfilling motherhood journey for ourselves and our children. So, let go, have fun and allow your children to bring out the inner child within you.

Reconnecting with nature allows us to tap into its soothing and rejuvenating energy. Take the time to go for walks in the park, hike in the mountains or simply sit by a peaceful lake.

NURTURING THE SOUL IN NATURE

Exploring the healing power of mother earth

In the hustle and bustle of modern motherhood, finding moments of peace and connection with nature is essential for both moms and children. Nature has a unique ability to nurture our souls, energise our atoms and provide profound opportunities for growth and learning. In this chapter, we delve into the healing power of Mother Earth and the transformative experiences that await us when we venture into the great outdoors.

RECONNECTING WITH THE NATURAL WORLD

As human beings, we are intrinsically connected to the natural world. However, the demands of modern life often lead us to lose touch with this vital connection. Reconnecting with nature allows us to tap into its soothing and rejuvenating energy. Take the time to go for walks in the park, hike in the mountains or simply sit by a peaceful lake. As you immerse yourself in the beauty and serenity of the natural world, you will feel a deep sense of connection and restoration.

THE HEALING POWER OF NATURE

Nature has a remarkable ability to heal and restore our wellbeing. Its sights, sounds and smells have a calming effect on our senses, reducing stress and anxiety. Research has shown that spending time in nature can improve our mood, boost our immune system and enhance our overall mental and physical health. By immersing ourselves and our children in the healing power of nature, we create a nurturing environment for growth and wellbeing.

LEARNING FROM THE WISDOM OF MOTHER EARTH

Nature is a wise teacher, offering valuable lessons and insights for both moms and children. Observe the intricate web of life, the balance of ecosystems and the resilience of plants and animals. Teach your children about the importance of environmental stewardship, cultivating a deep respect and appreciation for the natural world. Encourage them to explore, ask questions and discover the wonders of nature firsthand. By embracing nature as our classroom, we instil in our children a lifelong love for the Earth and a sense of responsibility towards its preservation.

UNPLUGGING AND EMBRACING SIMPLICITY

In our digital age, it is easy to become consumed by screens and technology. Nature provides a welcome respite from the constant barrage of notifications and distractions. When we venture into the outdoors, we have the opportunity to unplug and embrace simplicity. Leave behind the devices and immerse yourself in the beauty of the natural world. Encourage your children to engage their senses fully, listen to the sounds of birds chirping, feel the breeze on their skin, and marvel at the intricate patterns of leaves. By embracing simplicity, we cultivate a sense of presence and connection with the world around us.

BONDING IN NATURE

Nature offers the perfect backdrop for bonding and creating lasting memories with our children. Plan outdoor adventures, such as camping trips, nature walks or picnics in the park. Engage in activities that foster teamwork and cooperation, such as building a fort or planting a garden together. By sharing these experiences in nature, we strengthen our bonds with our children and create cherished moments of connection and joy.

CULTIVATING A SUSTAINABLE LIFESTYLE

Spending time in nature also inspires us to adopt a more sustainable lifestyle. As we witness the beauty and fragility of the natural world, we develop a deep sense of responsibility to protect it for future generations. Encourage your children to practice eco-friendly habits, such as recycling, conserving water and reducing waste. Teach them about the interconnectedness of all living things and the impact of our choices on the environment. By instilling these values, we equip our children with the tools to be conscious stewards of the Earth.

Venturing into nature nourishes our souls, energises us and provides invaluable opportunities for growth and learning. By reconnecting with the natural world, embracing its healing power, learning from its wisdom, unplugging and embracing simplicity, bonding with our children and cultivating a sustainable lifestyle, we embark on a transformative journey that enriches both our lives and the world around us. So, lace up your hiking boots, breathe in the fresh air and let Mother Earth nurture your soul and energise your spirit.

Our children need to know that there are certain limits in place to keep them safe and guide their actions.

NURTURING GROWTH AND SELF-DISCOVERY

The power of realistic boundaries

As mothers, we naturally want the best for our children. We may have dreams and expectations for them, hoping to see them excel and flourish in every aspect of their lives. However, it is important to recognise that the weight of excessive expectations can hinder their growth and connection to self. In this chapter, we explore the significance of setting realistic boundaries that allow our children to discover who they truly are within a safe and sacred space.

UNDERSTANDING EXPECTATIONS AND BOUNDARIES

Expectations are the beliefs and hopes we hold for our children's future. While it is natural to have aspirations for our children, it is important to differentiate between healthy aspirations and unrealistic expectations. Boundaries, on the other hand, are guidelines and limits that provide structure and safety. Realistic boundaries create a framework within which our children can explore their own identity and potentials.

FOSTERING SELF-DISCOVERY

By setting realistic boundaries, we create an environment where our children can engage in self-discovery. It is crucial to provide them with the freedom to explore their interests, talents and passions. Allow them to make choices and decisions, encouraging autonomy and independence. By doing so, we enable them to discover their unique strengths and preferences, laying the foundation for a fulfilling and authentic life journey.

A SAFE SACRED SPACE

Boundaries act as a protective container, providing a safe and sacred space for our children to navigate the world. By establishing clear boundaries, we create a sense of security and stability. Our children need to know that there are certain limits in place to keep them safe and guide their actions. Within these boundaries, they can confidently explore, make mistakes and learn valuable life lessons.

STEPPING OUTSIDE THE COMFORT ZONE

True growth often happens when we step outside our comfort zone, and the same applies to our children. While it is essential to provide a safe space, we should also encourage them to venture slightly beyond their comfort zone. This can be done by gently challenging them to try new experiences, take calculated risks and embrace uncertainty. By doing so, we nurture their resilience, adaptability and courage, enabling them to thrive in a rapidly changing world.

HONOURING INDIVIDUALITY

Each child is unique, with their own dreams, talents and aspirations. It is crucial to honour their individuality and support their personal journey.

Avoid imposing your own expectations and desires onto them. Instead, listen attentively, validate their feelings and interests and encourage them to pursue their passions authentically. By honouring their individuality, we empower them to become self-confident individuals who trust their own intuition and follow their hearts.

MAINTAINING BALANCE

Setting realistic boundaries requires finding a delicate balance between providing guidance and allowing freedom. While it is important to give our children room to explore and make their own choices, we must also provide guidance and support when needed. Pay attention to their developmental stages and adjust boundaries accordingly. As they grow, allow them to take on increasing responsibilities and gradually expand their boundaries.

EMBRACING MISTAKES AND LEARNING OPPORTUNITIES

Mistakes are an inevitable part of the learning process, and it is essential to create an environment where our children feel safe to make them. Encourage a growth mindset that views mistakes as valuable learning opportunities rather than failures. Teach them resilience, problem-solving skills and the importance of perseverance. By embracing mistakes and learning opportunities, we instil in them a lifelong love for learning and personal growth.

Setting boundaries in parenting is a powerful tool for nurturing our children's growth, self-confidence and resilience. It allows them to explore their identity, passions and potentials while providing the necessary structure and guidance. By fostering self-discovery, maintaining balance and embracing mistakes, we create a safe and sacred space where our children can thrive and become the best versions of themselves. As parents, we have the privilege and responsibility to set these boundaries with love, understanding and the belief in our children's limitless potential.

When a mother aligns her actions with her passions, a deep sense of fulfilment takes root within her being.

MOMS ON A MISSION

Finding happiness and health

In the realm of motherhood, there exists a profound truth: moms who embark on a mission are not only happier but also healthier. When a mother discovers her purpose and passion, she taps into a wellspring of joy and vitality that positively impacts every aspect of her life.

I know that this was definitely the case for me! I knew the moment that I discovered the power of story that I would never be able to step back from the mission I was called to. To see my work making a real difference in others' lives lights me up. And to be able to pursue it aligned with being a hands-on mom, well that means I am aligned with my values of not compromising my motherhood role.

A few key things that can help in the pursuit of health and happiness are:

MISSION AND PURPOSE

The key to happiness: A mother on a mission is a mother who has discovered her purpose beyond the daily responsibilities of caring for her children. This mission could be pursuing a career, engaging in a creative pursuit, championing a cause or any endeavour that ignites her soul. When a mother aligns her actions with her passions, a deep sense of fulfilment takes root within her being.

HAPPINESS RADIATES

The ripple effect: When a mother is happy and fulfilled, her positive energy radiates to those around her. Her children witness a role model who embraces life with enthusiasm, resilience and a zest for learning. This happiness becomes contagious, shaping the emotional wellbeing of the entire family. A joyful mother creates a harmonious environment that nurtures the growth and happiness of her children.

HEALTH BENEFITS

Mind, body and spirit: A mother on a mission experiences a myriad of health benefits that extend beyond mere happiness. The mind becomes sharper and more focused as she engages in activities that stimulate her intellect and creativity. The body gains strength and vitality as she pursues physical endeavours aligned with her passion. The spirit soars as she connects with something greater than herself, finding purpose and meaning in her journey.

BALANCE AND SELF-CARE

The foundation of health: To fully embrace their mission, mothers must prioritise self-care and maintain a delicate balance in their lives. This involves setting boundaries, delegating tasks and carving out time for personal rejuvenation. By caring for themselves, mothers replenish their energy reserves, allowing them to serve their mission with renewed vigor and enthusiasm.

EMBRACING IMPERFECTIONS

The path to self-acceptance: On the journey of motherhood, there will be moments of challenge and imperfection. Yet, mothers on a mission understand that it is through these experiences that growth and learning occur. They embrace their flaws and mistakes as opportunities for growth rather than dwelling on self-judgement. This acceptance fosters resilience, self-compassion and an unwavering belief in their ability to overcome any obstacle.

BUILDING A SUPPORTIVE NETWORK

Allies on the mission: Mothers on a mission understand the importance of building a supportive network around them. They seek out like-minded individuals who inspire and uplift them. They surround themselves with people who understand their passions and dreams, offering encouragement and support. These allies become an invaluable source of strength and motivation on the journey.

REALIGNING WITH THE MISSION

Navigating transitions: As seasons of motherhood change and children grow, a mother's mission may evolve as well. Mothers on a mission understand the need for periodic self-reflection and realignment. They embrace the shifting tides, adapting their purpose and passions to align with their changing circumstances. This flexibility ensures that their happiness and health remain steadfast even amidst the ebb and flow of life.

In the realm of motherhood, a mother on a mission can discover the path to happiness and health. By embracing her purpose, nurturing her wellbeing and finding balance, she becomes a beacon of joy and vitality, positively impacting the lives of her children and those around her. Wouldn't it be amazing if mothers embarked on their unique missions, unlocking the true essence of their happiness and wellbeing!

Self-mastery involves taking ownership of our lives, emotions and actions.

STABILITY AND SELF-MASTERY

Being the rock for our children

As mothers, one of the greatest gifts we can give our children is the stability and self-mastery that comes from having our lives in order. When we have a solid foundation and maintain a sense of balance, our children can rely on us as a stable base from which they can explore the world and navigate their own journeys. In this chapter, we delve into the importance of stability and self-mastery in our role as mothers and how it positively impacts our children's lives.

THE POWER OF STABILITY

Stability provides a sense of security and consistency that is vital for our children's wellbeing. When our lives are organised, predictable and grounded, our children feel safe and reassured. Stability allows them to develop trust, form healthy attachments and explore the world with confidence. By being a stable presence, we offer our children a solid foundation from which they can grow, learn and flourish.

CREATING ORDER AND ROUTINE

Creating order and routine in our daily lives establishes a sense of structure and predictability for our children. Having regular meal times, consistent bedtimes and established routines for daily activities helps our children feel grounded and secure. By maintaining a sense of order, we create an environment where our children know what to expect and can develop a sense of responsibility and independence.

EMOTIONAL STABILITY

In addition to external stability, emotional stability is equally important for our children's wellbeing. When we regulate our emotions and respond to situations with calmness and mindfulness, we teach our children valuable skills for emotional self-regulation. By modelling emotional stability, we show them that challenges can be managed, emotions can be understood and expressed in healthy ways and conflicts can be resolved peacefully.

SELF-MASTERY AS A ROLE MODEL

Self-mastery involves taking ownership of our lives, emotions and actions. As mothers, practicing self-mastery allows us to be role models for our children. When we demonstrate self-discipline, resilience and self-care, we teach our children the importance of personal responsibility and self-growth. By mastering our own lives, we inspire our children to take charge of their own journeys and develop the skills necessary for success and fulfilment.

BALANCING MOTHERHOOD AND SELF-CARE

Maintaining stability and self-mastery requires finding a healthy balance between our role as mothers and our own self-care. It is crucial to prioritise our own wellbeing, physical and mental health and personal interests. By nourishing ourselves, we recharge our energy, reduce stress and enhance our ability to be present and engaged with our children. Finding time for self-care and pursuing our passions allows us to show up as the best version of ourselves for our children.

SEEKING SUPPORT

Achieving stability and self-mastery does not mean we have to do it all alone. Seeking support from our partners, family, friends and community is essential. Building a strong support network provides us with the resources, encouragement and help we need to maintain stability in our lives. By surrounding ourselves with positive influences and seeking support when needed, we create a nurturing environment for ourselves and our children.

Being a stable base and having our lives in order is a profound gift we can offer our children. By creating stability, establishing routines, nurturing emotional wellbeing, practicing self-mastery and balancing motherhood with self-care, we become the rock that our children can depend on. Let us strive to cultivate stability and self-mastery, recognising the positive impact it has on our children's lives as they navigate the world with confidence, resilience and a deep sense of security.

NAVIGATING MOTHERHOOD'S EMOTIONAL LANDSCAPE

Finding balance and cultivating inner peace

Motherhood is a beautiful and transformative journey filled with moments of joy, love and fulfilment. However, it can also be emotionally challenging, leaving us feeling exhausted, overwhelmed and even conflicted at times. In this chapter, we explore the different emotional states we may experience as moms – the peaceful zen mom, the impulsive mom and the cross mom. We delve into the importance of finding balance, cultivating inner peace and embracing self-compassion while navigating the complexities of motherhood.

THE PEACEFUL ZEN MOM

Cultivating calmness: Explore practices that help you cultivate inner peace and maintain a sense of calmness amidst the chaos of daily life.

Incorporate mindfulness, meditation, deep breathing exercises or gentle movement to find moments of tranquility.

Embracing self-care: Prioritise self-care as a means of nourishing your body, mind and spirit. Engage in activities that bring you joy, relaxation and rejuvenation, allowing yourself to recharge and restore your inner balance.

Setting boundaries: Learn to set healthy boundaries and say no when necessary. Understand that your wellbeing is essential and that taking care of yourself allows you to show up fully for your children.

THE IMPULSIVE MOM

Managing impulsive reactions: Recognise impulsive reactions that may arise due to stress or exhaustion. Practice pausing and taking a moment before responding, allowing yourself to respond consciously rather than impulsively.

Seeking support: Reach out for support when needed. Connect with other moms, friends or professionals who can provide guidance, under-standing and a fresh perspective. Remember that asking for help is a sign of strength, not weakness.

Practicing self-compassion: Be kind and gentle with yourself when you make mistakes or have impulsive reactions. Remember that you are human and it's natural to experience moments of frustration or impa-tience. Embrace self-forgiveness and learn from these experiences to grow and evolve as a mom.

THE CROSS MOM

Understanding triggers and stressors: Identify the triggers and stressors that may lead to feelings of anger, frustration or impatience. Explore strategies to manage these triggers, such as taking breaks, engaging in stress-relieving activities or seeking professional support if needed.

Embracing emotional regulation techniques: Learn techniques for emotional regulation, such as deep breathing, journalling or engaging in activities that help you process and release emotions in a healthy way. Find what works for you and incorporate these practices into your daily life.

Cultivating self-awareness: Practice self-reflection and self-awareness to understand the root causes of your cross moments. Explore any underlying emotions, beliefs or unresolved issues that may contribute to these reactions. Seek support or therapy if necessary to address and heal these deeper issues.

Motherhood is a journey of constant growth and self-discovery, filled with a range of emotions and experiences. While it's natural to experience moments of impatience, frustration or exhaustion, it is important to find balance and cultivate inner peace amidst the challenges. By embracing practices that promote calmness, setting healthy boundaries, seeking support, practicing self-compassion and developing emotional regulation techniques, we can navigate the emotional landscape of motherhood with grace and authenticity. Remember that you are a loving mom, and even in your most challenging moments, there is love in your heart. Embrace self-care, seek support and find solace in the knowledge that you are doing your best.

Rituals and traditions provide a sense of belonging and create lasting memories.

TIME IS OF THE ESSENCE

Nurturing with attention, not just money

In our busy lives, it's easy to get caught up in the hustle and bustle, thinking that providing for our children financially is the most important thing. However, what our children truly crave is not just our money but our genuine presence and attention. In this chapter, we explore the significance of time in parenting and how nurturing our children with attention can create deep and meaningful connections. By recognising that time is of the essence, we can prioritise quality moments with our children and truly meet their emotional needs.

QUALITY TIME OVER QUANTITY

The importance of presence: Being physically present is not enough; we must also be mentally and emotionally present for our children. Quality time is about giving our undivided attention, listening actively and engaging in meaningful interactions.

Making the most of limited time: It's not always about the quantity of time we spend with our children but the quality of those moments.

Even short, focused interactions can have a significant impact on their emotional wellbeing.

CREATING MEANINGFUL RITUALS

Establishing family traditions: Rituals and traditions provide a sense of belonging and create lasting memories. Establish regular family activities, such as game nights, movie nights or weekly outings, that allow for bonding and connection.

Daily rituals: Incorporate simple daily rituals, like sharing meals together, bedtime routines or morning conversations, that create a consistent space for connection and communication.

ACTIVE LISTENING AND COMMUNICATION

Practice active listening: Truly listening to our children without judgement or interruption shows them that we value their thoughts and feelings. Create a safe space for open and honest communication, allowing them to express themselves freely.

Validate their emotions: Acknowledge and validate their emotions, even if they differ from our own. Help them understand and process their feelings, fostering emotional intelligence and trust.

UNPLUGGED PARENTING

Limiting screen time: Set boundaries around screen time for both you and your children. Allocate designated tech-free periods to engage in meaningful activities and conversations, promoting face-to-face interactions.

Be present in the moment: Put away distractions, such as phones or work-related tasks, and fully engage with your children. Show them that they have your undivided attention and that they are a priority in your life.

CREATING BALANCE

Time management: Prioritise your time to find a balance between work, personal responsibilities and parenting. Evaluate your commitments and make intentional choices to allocate time for your children.

Self-care: Remember to take care of yourself, as your wellbeing directly affects your ability to be present for your children. Prioritising self-care allows you to recharge and be fully present when you are with them.

EMBRACING SPONTANEITY

Seizing opportunities: Be open to spontaneous moments with your children. Embrace impromptu adventures, playtime or conversations that arise naturally. These unexpected moments can create beautiful memories and strengthen your connection.

While financial support is important, it's our genuine presence and attention that our children truly crave. Time is a precious gift that allows us to nurture deep and meaningful connections with our children. By prioritising quality time over quantity, creating meaningful rituals, practicing active listening, unplugging from distractions and finding balance, we can show our children that they are valued and loved. Remember, time is of the essence, and investing it in our children will yield immeasurable rewards in their emotional wellbeing and the strength of our parent-child bond.

Sustaining the magic of life throughout motherhood requires a conscious and intentional approach.

SUSTAINING THE MAGIC

Embracing the journey of motherhood

Throughout this book, we have explored the transformative power of life magic mastery for moms. We have delved into the universal laws and the seven life principles of mindfulness, knowing, intention, love, gratitude, forgiveness and belief. These chapters have provided insights, practices and guidance for embracing the magic within motherhood and cultivating a life filled with joy, abundance and purpose. In this concluding chapter, we will reflect on the journey we have embarked upon and explore strategies for sustaining the magic of life throughout motherhood in a sustainable and fulfilling way.

REFLECTING ON THE JOURNEY

Celebrating growth and progress: Take a moment to acknowledge and celebrate how far you have come in your motherhood journey. Recognise the personal growth, resilience and wisdom you have gained along the way.

Embracing the ebb and flow: Motherhood is a journey of constant change and evolution. Embrace the ebb and flow of life, knowing that each phase brings its own unique gifts and challenges.

FINDING SUSTAINABLE BALANCE

Self-care as a non-negotiable: Prioritise self-care as an essential part of your daily routine. Nurture your physical, emotional and mental wellbeing to sustain your energy and ability to show up fully for yourself and your children.

Setting boundaries and practicing saying no: Learn to set healthy boundaries and say no to commitments that do not align with your priorities and values. Create space for the activities and relationships that bring you joy and fulfillment.

CULTIVATING A SUPPORTIVE COMMUNITY

Connecting with like-minded mothers: Surround yourself with a supportive community of like-minded mothers who understand and share your journey. Share experiences, insights and challenges, and find solace in the understanding and empathy of others.

Seeking professional support when needed: Do not hesitate to seek professional support if you find yourself overwhelmed or struggling. Therapists, coaches or support groups can provide guidance and help you navigate the complexities of motherhood.

LIVING WITH INTENTION

Revisiting your vision and purpose: Regularly revisit your vision and purpose as a mother. Align your actions and decisions with your intentions to create a meaningful and purposeful motherhood journey.

Practicing presence and mindfulness: Cultivate the practice of mindfulness and presence in your interactions with your children. Embrace the beauty and magic of each moment, cherishing the connections and experiences that unfold.

NURTURING YOUR INNER CHILD

Embracing playfulness and joy: Allow your inner child to come out and play alongside your children. Embrace the joy, wonder and curiosity that children naturally possess, and let it infuse your daily life with lightness and laughter.

Finding balance between responsibilities and fun: Strive to find a balance between the responsibilities of motherhood and the need for fun and spontaneity. Create opportunities for adventure, exploration and shared experiences with your children.

EMBRACING IMPERFECTION AND GROWTH

Letting go of perfectionism: Release the need for perfection and embrace the beauty of imperfection. Understand that growth and learning occur through the inevitable challenges and mistakes that arise in motherhood.

Cultivating a growth mindset: Foster a growth mindset in yourself and your children, recognising that setbacks and failures are opportunities for learning and growth. Encourage resilience, perseverance and a positive attitude towards challenges.

Sustaining the magic of life throughout motherhood requires a conscious and intentional approach. By reflecting on the journey, finding balance, cultivating support, living with intention, nurturing your inner child and embracing imperfection and growth, you can harness the transformative power of motherhood in a sustainable and fulfilling way. Embrace each day with love, grace and gratitude, knowing that you are creating a legacy of love and magic for yourself and your children. May your motherhood journey be a testament to the infinite possibilities that arise when we embrace the magic within and live authentically as mothers.

Bringing It All Together

Through love, mindfulness, gratitude and unwavering belief, mothers become beacons of light, guiding their children towards a future filled with love, purpose and limitless potential.

Presented in the sections of Awakening, Universal Thinking, Life Magic Mastery Gifts, Mindfulness, Knowing, Intention, Love, Gratitude, Forgiveness, Belief and Motherhood Superpower collectively illuminate the extraordinary journey of motherhood and the profound impact it has on both mothers and their children. Each article explores different facets of motherhood, offering insights, guidance and practical tools for mothers to embrace their role with love, purpose and empowerment.

Through the process of awakening, mothers are encouraged to tap into their inner wisdom, recognising their innate power and embracing their unique gifts. The articles emphasise the importance of universal thinking, highlighting the interconnectedness of all beings and the ripple effect of a mother's actions, thoughts and intentions.

The concept of Life Magic Mastery Gifts introduces the idea that mothers possess extraordinary abilities to create and manifest positive change in their lives and the lives of their children. By cultivating mindfulness, mothers learn to be fully present in each moment, fostering deeper connections, and experiencing the magic of motherhood in its purest form.

Knowing and intuition are celebrated as invaluable tools for mothers, guiding them in making decisions and providing the necessary guidance and support for their children. The articles emphasise the power of setting intentions and leveraging the law of attraction to create miracles in motherhood and beyond.

Love, gratitude and forgiveness are explored as transformative forces in a mother's life, nurturing deep connections, fostering emotional freedom and creating a nurturing environment for both mother and child. Belief in oneself and in the potential of one's child is highlighted as foundational gold, empowering children to embrace their worth and pursue their dreams fearlessly.

Collectively, these articles present a comprehensive guide for mothers to harness their superpowers and embrace the journey of motherhood with grace, strength and joy. They offer practical strategies, personal anecdotes and timeless wisdom to inspire and support mothers in navigating the challenges and joys of raising children.

In the realm of motherhood, the possibilities are boundless. As mothers embrace their superpowers and tap into the magic of life, they not only transform their own lives but also create a profound impact on the world around them. Through love, mindfulness, gratitude and unwavering belief, mothers become beacons of light, guiding their children towards a future filled with love, purpose and limitless potential.

Karen Weaver is a multi-award-winning entrepreneur and author and the founder of Serenity Press, MMH Press, KMD Books, and Duchess Serenity Press.

She is a multi-genre author of over 40 books, a Forbes influencer, a 3x TEDx speaker, and a proud mum of 6.   She's an advanced Law of Attraction practitioner who teaches people how to attract anything they want into their lives and writes about her success principles as K P Weaver.

Her annual retreats are sought-after events with featured famous guests and are hosted in an Irish castle.

Her motto is: Where there is a will there is always a way.

Her quote is: When time and circumstance align, magic happens.

Karen is passionate about sharing her extensive knowledge and vibrant energy with others. She has a 'no excuse' policy: if she can do it, anyone can!   She believes in the power of mums in business leading the way for the next generation to live to their highest potential. Karen is on a mission to share the power of stories with the world.

Books &
courses
Coming
2023

www.kpweaver.com

www.ingramcontent.com/pod-product-compliance
Lightning Source LLC
Chambersburg PA
CBHW021243060726
47590CB00005B/1879